French - Marathi

LEARNING FLASHCARDS

FOR BABIES TODDLERS

alligator

मगरमच्छ

The alligator is having a party.

fourmi

मुंगी

The ant is red.

ours

अस्वल

The bear loves you.

abeille

मधमाशी

The bee is saying hello.

oiseau

पक्षी

The bird is flying.

papillon

फुलपाखरू

The butterfly is pretty.

chameau

उंट

The camel has a hump.

chat

मांजर

The cat is happy.

dinosaure

डायनासोर

The dinosaur is laying eggs.

poulet

कोंबडी

The chicken is dancing.

vache

गाय

The cow has a bell.

cerf

हरिण

The reindeer has a toy.

chien

कुत्रा

The dog has two floppy ears.

dauphin

डॉल्फिन

The dolphin is swimming.

canard

बदक

The duck has a bow.

aigle

गरुड

The eagle is looking for food.

l'éléphant

हत्ती

The elephant is sitting.

poisson

मासे

The fish is a clownfish.

libellule

डॅगनफ्लाय

The dragonfly is blue.

renard

कोल्हा

The fox has a red nose.

grenouille

बेडूक

The frog is smiling.

girafe

जिराफ

The giraffe has a long neck.

chèvre

शेळी

The goat has a beard

ver de terre

जंत

The worm is in the apple

poule

कोंबडी

The hen has chicks.

hippopotame

हिप्पोपोटॅमस

The hippo is big.

cheval

घोडा

The horse is fast.

kangourou

कांगारू

The kangaroo has a baby.

chaton

मांजरीचे पिल्लू

The kitten is playing.

lion

सिंह

The lion has a mane.

homard

लॉबस्टर

The lobster is red.

singe

माकड

The monkey has a tail.

poulpe

आठ पायांचा सागरी प्राणी

The octopus has food.

hibou

घुबड

The owls have big eyes.

panda

पांडा

The panda wears a diaper.

porc

डुक्कर

The pig is fat and pink.

chiot

गर्विष्ठ तरुण

The dog is brown.

lapin

ससा

The rabbit has a carrot.

rat

उंदीर

The mouse is writing something.

crabe

खेकडा

The crab has two pinchers.

requin

शार्क

The shark is scary.

mouton

मेंढी

The sheep are very fluffy.

escargot

गोगलगाय

The snail is slow.

serpent

साप

The snake has poison.

araignée

कोळी

The spider is purple.

écureuil

गिलहरी

The squirrel has a nut.

tigre

वाघ

The tiger has a red bow.

tortue

कासव

The turtle has a shell.

loup

लांडगा

The wolf is smiling.

zèbre

झेब्रा

The zebra is black and white.

dinde

टर्की

The turkey has two legs.

coq

कोंबडी

The rooster will crow.

perroquet

पोपट

The parrot is colorful.

hérisson

हेजहोग

The hedgehog has apples.

pomme

सफरचंद

The apple has a leaf.

abricot

जर्दाळू

The apricot is yellow.

avocat

एवोकॅडो

The avocado has a nut.

banane

केळी

The banana is yellow.

la mûre

ब्लॅकबेरी

There are a lot of blackberries.

cassis

काळ्या रंगाचा

The blackcurrants are yummy.

myrtille

ब्लूबेरी

The blueberries are sweet.

cerise

चेरी

The cherries have a stem.

noix de coco

नारळ

The coconuts have juice.

figues

अंजीर

The fig has seeds.

grain de raisin

द्राक्ष

The grapes are purple.

pamplemousse

द्राक्षफळ

The grapefruits are sour.

kiwi

किवी

The kiwi is fresh.

citron

लिंबृ

The lemons are yellow.

citron vert

चुना

We have lots of lime.

litchi

लीची

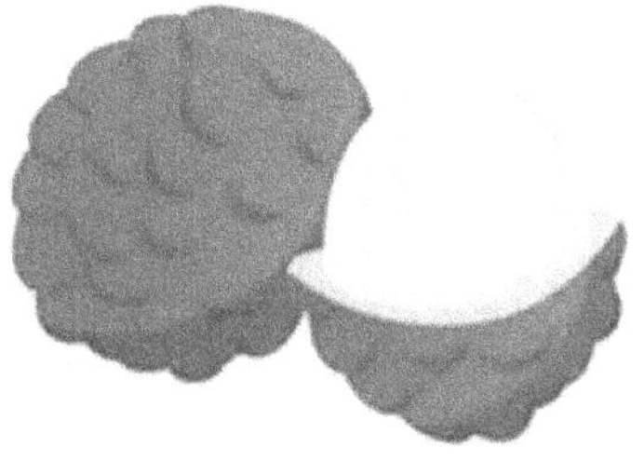

I like to eat lychee.

mandarine

मंदारिन केशरी

Oranges are refreshing.

mangue

आंबा

Mango is my favorite fruit.

orange

केशरी

Mandarins are like oranges.

papaye

पपई

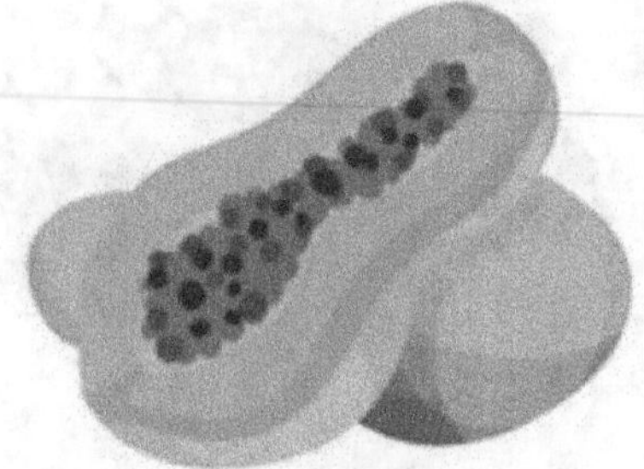

Papayas have lots of seeds.

pêche

सुदंर आकर्षक मुलगी

Peaches are juicy.

poire

pear

Pears have a strange figure.

ananas

अननस

The pineapple has a thumbs up.

prune

मनुका

Plums are healthy for you.

grenade

डाळिंब

Pomegranates are all red.

framboise

तिरस्कारदर्शक किंवा नापसंतीदर्शक हावभाव

The raspberry is shiny.

fraise

छोटी

The strawberry has leaves on top.

pastèque

टरबूज

The watermelon is big.

mandarine

टेंजरिन

The tangerine looks like an orange.

tarte

पाई

I like to eat apple pie.

gâteau

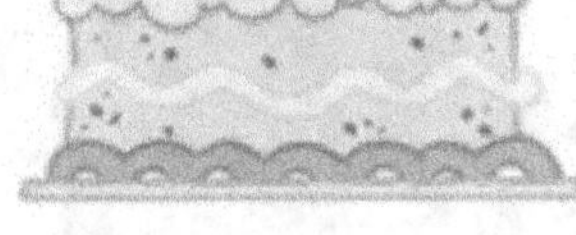

केक

That cake is huge.

bonbons

कँडी

Candy is not good for your teeth.

biscuit

कुकी

Cookies are easy to make.

donut

डोनट

I like strawberry donuts.

crème glacée

आईसक्रीम

The ice cream is melting.

muffin

मफिन

The muffin has a cute wrapper.

pudding

सांजा

We eat pudding on Christmas.

classeur

बाईंडर

I keep pictures in my binder.

livre

पुस्तक

I like to eat books.

sac à dos

बॅकपॅक

The backpack has lots of stuff.

les ciseaux

कात्री

I have scissors in my bag.

épingles

पिन

Pins can hold stuff up.

agrafe

क्लिप

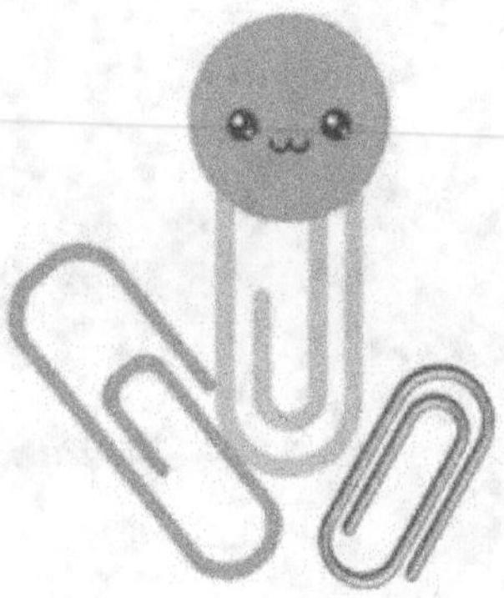

Clips can hold up paper.

papier

कागद

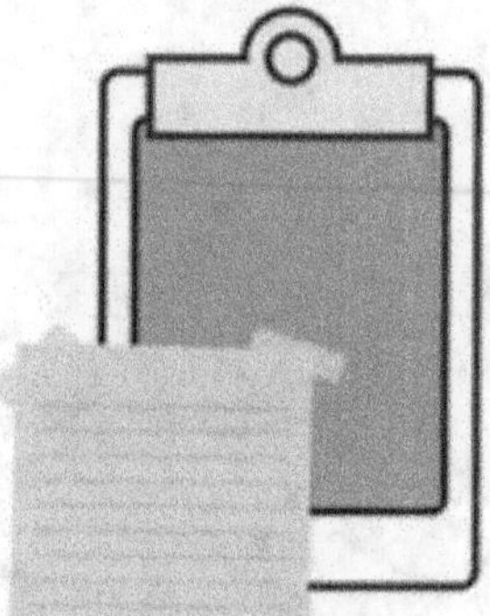

I have lots of paper.

agrafeuse

स्टेपलर

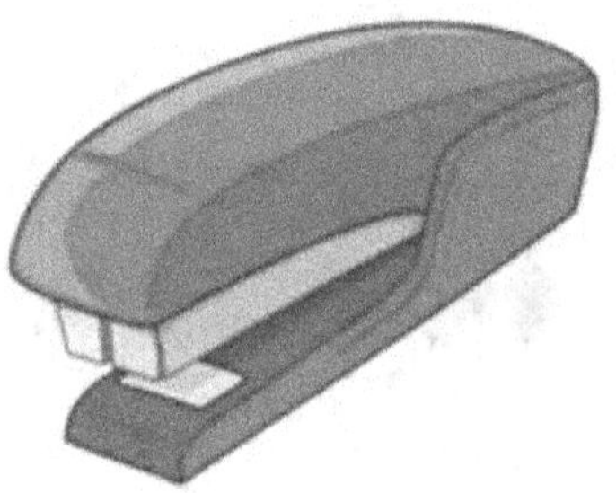

My stapler is shiny and red.

calculatrice

कॅल्क्युलेटर

My calculator has buttons.

règle

शासक

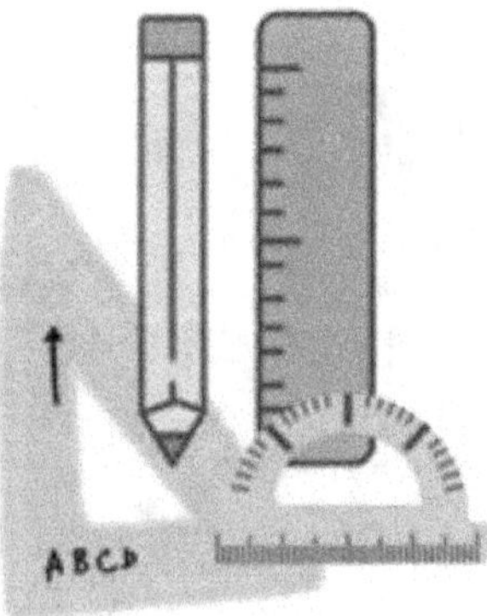

I have lots of rulers.

la colle

सरस

The glue is sticky.

bibliothèque

बुककेस

My bookcase has lots of things.

calendrier

कॅलेंडर

I have a calendar on my table.

chaise

खुर्ची

My chair is fancy.

l'horloge

घड्याळ

The clock says that it's 3 o'clock.

ordinateur

संगणक

I do things on my computer.

bureaux

डेस्क

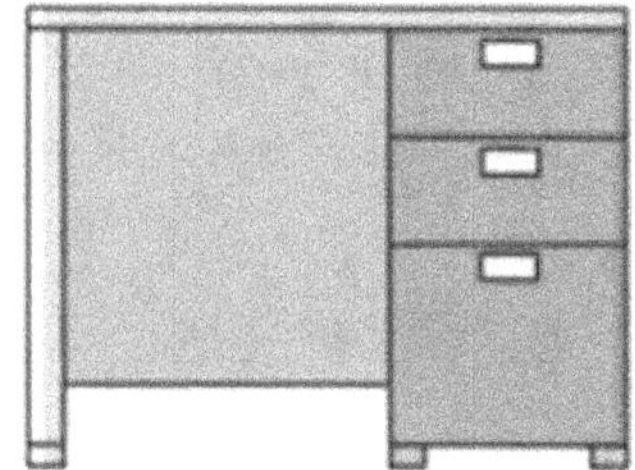

I put lots of things on my desk.

dictionnaire

शब्दकोश

The dictionary has lots of words.

la gomme

इरेजर

Erasers are used with pencils.

carte

नकाशा

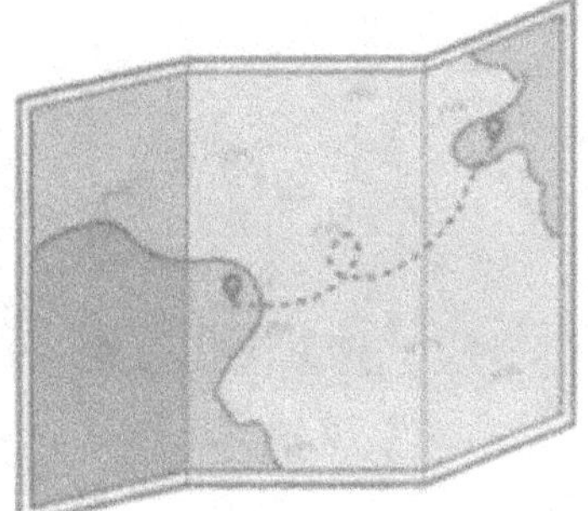

The map shows you different places.

carnet

नोटबुक

I use notebooks at school.

stylo

पेन

My pen is very pretty.

crayon

पेन्सिल

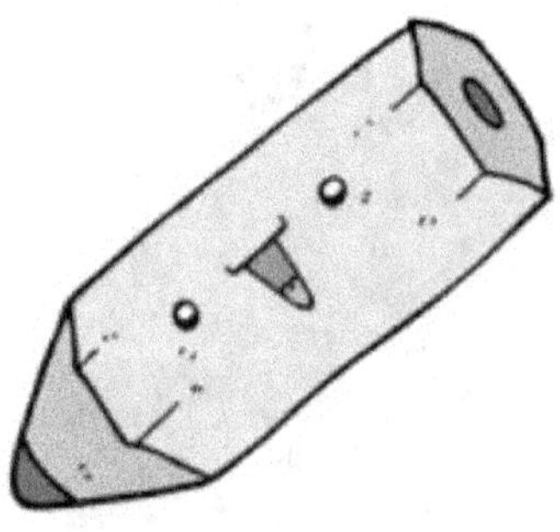

My friend gave me a pencil.

ceinture

बेल्ट

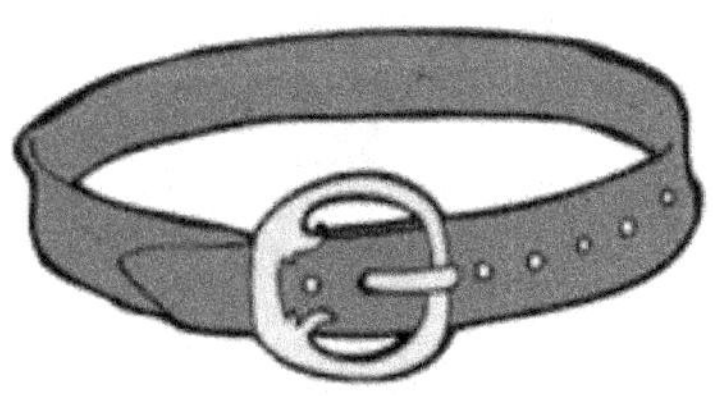

I have a belt on my pants.

bottes

बूट

I have big brown boots.

chapeau

टोपी

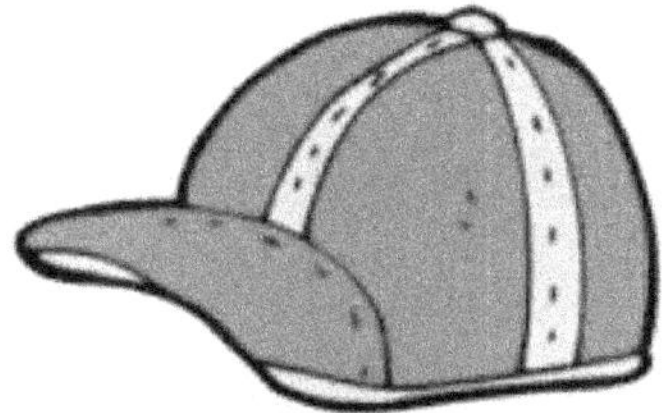

My mom bought me a new cap.

manteau

कोट

She has a long yellow coat.

robes

कपडे

My dress has a bow.

gants

हातमोजा

I got new gloves.

chapeau

टोपी

That hat is for a wicked witch.

veste

जाकीट

The jacket is cozy.

jeans

निव्ळ्या सुती कापड्याच्या विजारी

My jeans are long.

pyjamas

पायजामा

I sleep in my pajamas.

un pantalon

अर्धी चड्डी

The bear is wearing pants.

imperméable

रेनकोट

We wear our raincoats when it is raining.

écharpe

गळपट्टा

The baby has a scarf around his neck.

chemise

शर्ट

I like this shirt the best.

des chaussures

शूज

I have red and blue shoes.

jupe

परकर

My skirt has lots of buttons.

pantalon

स्लॅक्स

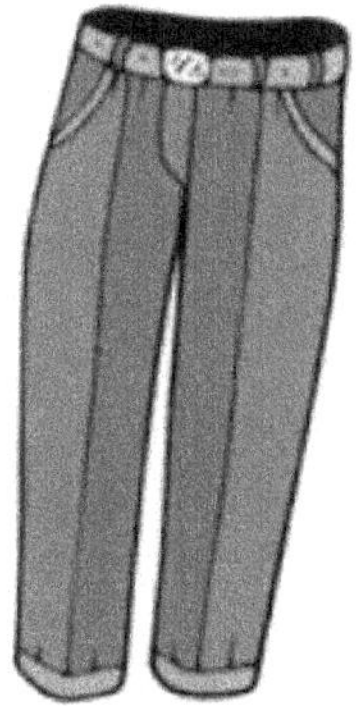

My dad wears slacks.

chaussons

चप्पल

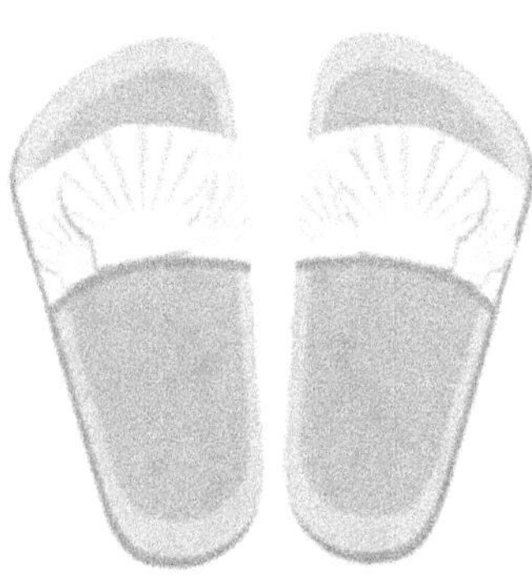

I have seashells on my sandals.

chaussettes

मोजे

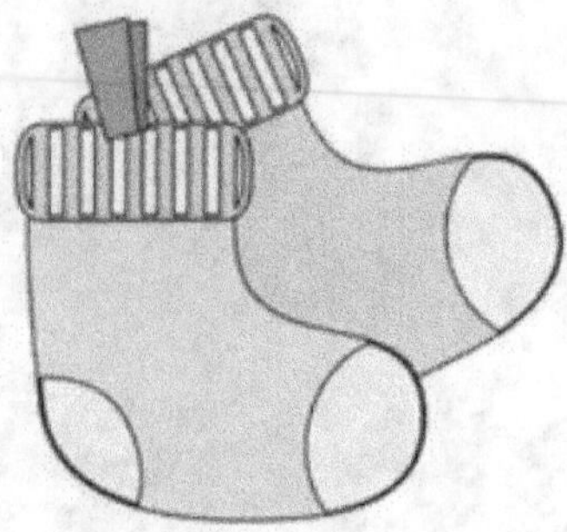

My baby sister wears socks.

costume

खटला

My brother is wearing a suit.

chandail

स्वेटर

I am wearing a sweater for winter.

cravate

नेकटी

My dad wears a tie to meetings.

pantalon

पायघोळ

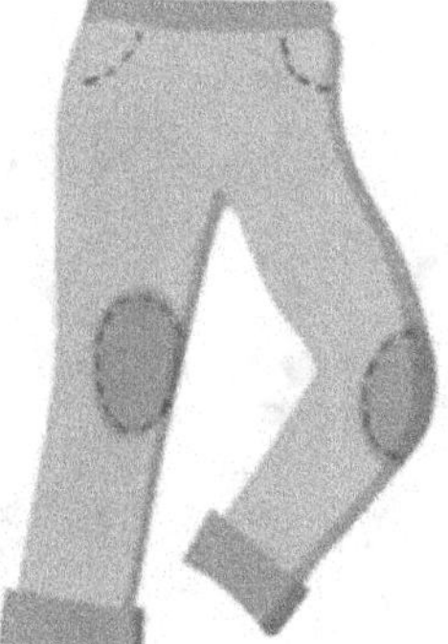

The trousers look like jeans.

slip

पायघोळ

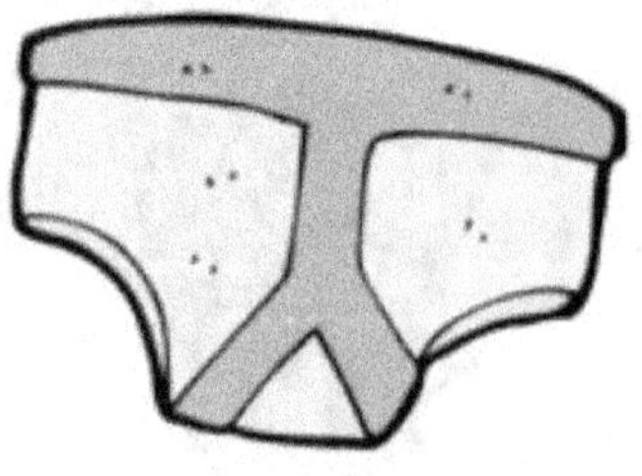

I always wear my underwear.

maillot de corps

अधोरेखित

My undershirt has a star.

une

एक

Number one and the bee are friends.

deux

दोन

The cat and the mouse both love two.

trois

तीन

The bear gives number three a present.

quatre

चार

Number four is a home for the cat.

cinq

पाच

Number five hatches an egg.

six

सहा

Number six is going to eat a carrot.

sept

सात

Number seven is playing with the tiger.

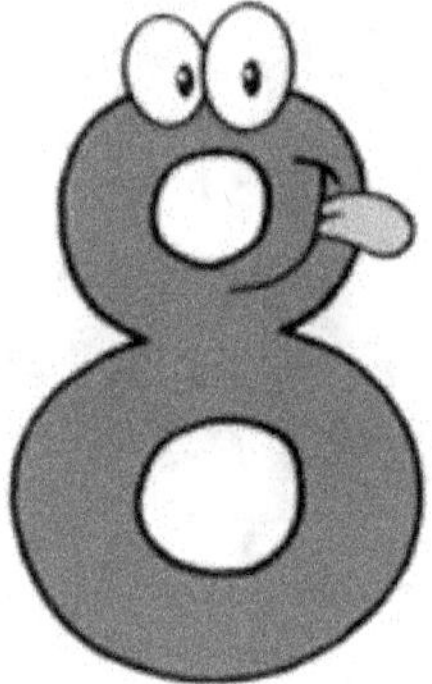

huit

आठ

Number eight is funny.

neuf

नऊ

Number nine meets the parrot.

dix

दहा

Number ten is smiling.

onze

अकरा

Number eleven has big eyes.

douze

बारा

Number twelve is number one and two.

treize

तेरा

Number thirteen is excited.

quatorze

चौदा

The number fourteen is vast.

quinze

पंधरा

The number fifteen is green.

seize

सोळा

Sixteen is my lucky number.

dix-sept

सतरा

Number seventeen look alike.

dix-huit

अठरा

Number eighteen will go to the circus.

dix-neuf

एकोणीस

I am nineteen now!

vingt

वीस

Number twenty has a zero.

fourmi

मुंगी

The ant has lots of legs.

cloche

घंटा

The bell will ring.

vache

गाय

The cow has a bow.

poupée

बाहुली

She has a cute bear doll.

oeuf

अंडी

The chick has hatched out of the egg.

poisson

मासे

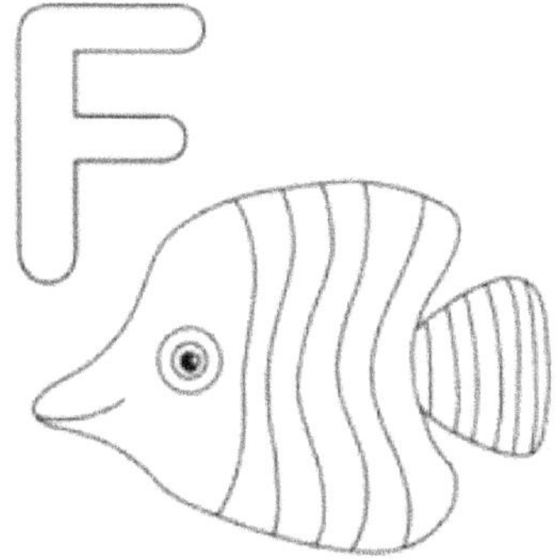

The fish is swimming in the water.

chèvre

शेळी

The goat is sitting on the grass.

chapeau

टोपी

He is wearing a hat.

crème glacée

आईसक्रीम

I like to eat ice cream.

confiture

ठप्प

The kitten is sitting on the jam jar.

chaton

मांजरीचे पिल्लृ

The cat is sleeping on the floor.

lion

सिंह

The lion is waiting for the tiger.

rat

उंदीर

The mouse has lots of presents.

nez

नाक

The reindeer has a red nose.

hibou

घुबड

The owl is sleeping.

porc

डुक्कर

The pig will eat cupcakes.

reine

राणी

The queen has a big crown.

lapin

ससा

The rabbit is jumping up and down.

mouton

मेंढी

The sheep have fluffy wool.

tortue

कासव

The turtle has a shell.

parapluie

छत्री

The mouse is holding an umbrella.

van

व्हॅन

The van is driving along the road.

pastèque

टरबूज

The watermelon has lots of seeds.

xylophone

xylophone

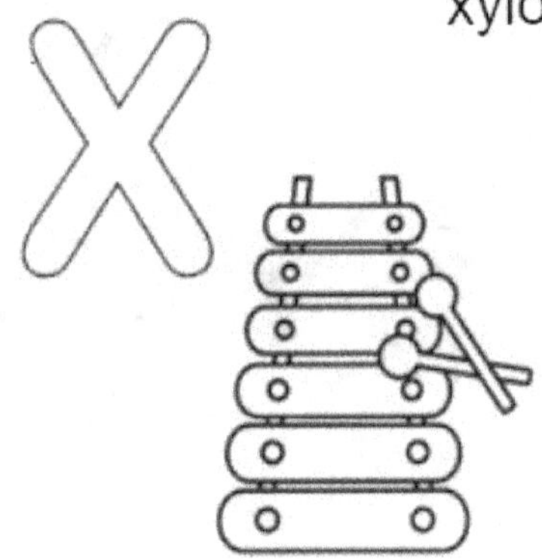

We are going to play the
xylophone.

yaourt

दही

We opened the yogurt can.

zèbre

झेब्रा

The zebra is surprised.

rose

गुलाबी

color the word and
the picture in pink

pink

Most of my clothes are pink.

marron

तपकिरी

color the word and
the picture in pink

brown

My chocolate is brown.

gris

राखाडी

color the word and
the picture in pink

gray

I don't like the color gray.

vert

हिरवा

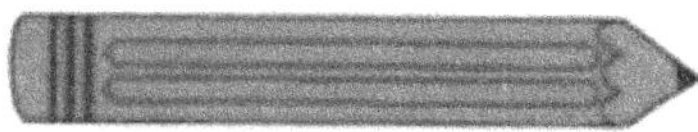

color the word and
the picture in pink

green

The vegetables are green.

jaune

पिवळा

color the word and
the picture in pink

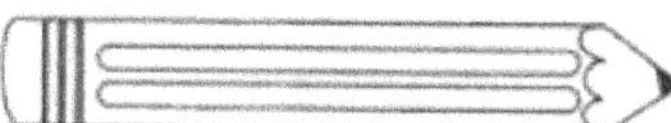

yellow

Bananas are yellow.

blanc

पांढरा

color the word and
the picture in pink

white

The paper that I write on is white.

rouge

लाल

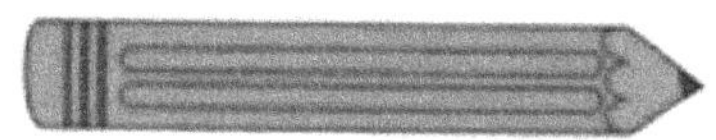

color the word and
the picture in pink

red

Apples are red.

bleu

निळा

color the word and
the picture in pink

The night sky is blue.

percer

धान्य पेरण्याचे यंत्र

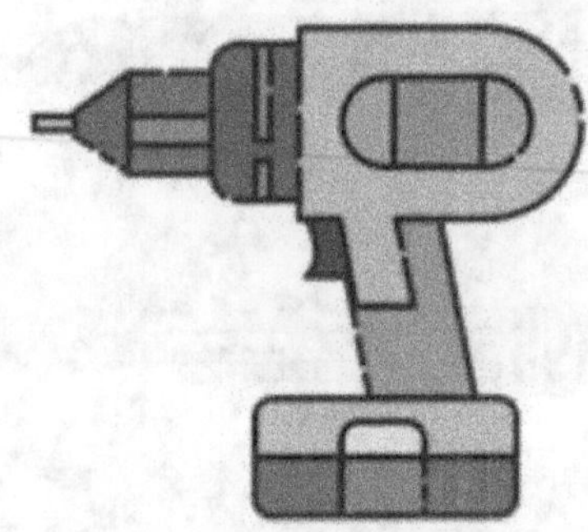

The drill will help us fix this.

marteau

हातोडा

The hammer is going to nail the
picture.

couteau

चाकू

The knife is sharp.

pinces

फिकट

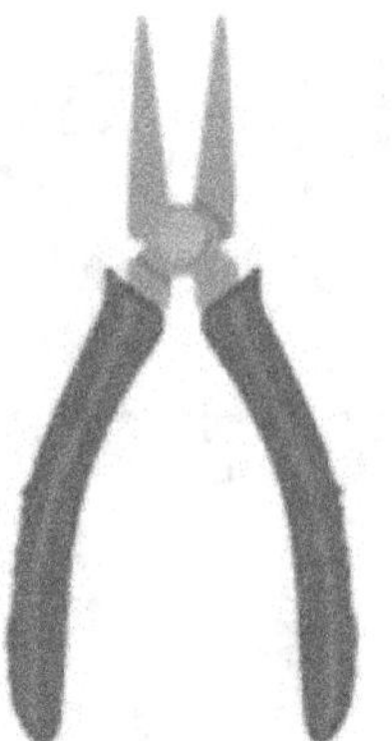

The plier is used for many things.

vu

पाहिले

The saw can chop wood.

les ciseaux

कात्री

I use scissors to cut paper.

tournevis

पेचकस

The screwdriver can screw in the knots.

clé

पाना

The wrench can help unscrew the knots.

avion

विमान

The airplane is going to leave now.

vélo

सायकल

The bicycle is beautiful.

bateau

बोट

The boat is floating on the water.

autobus

बस

The bus is going to school.

voiture

गाडी

The car is green.

hélicoptère

हेलिकॉप्टर

The helicopter is looking for something.

cheval

घोडा

You can ride the horse.

jet

जेट

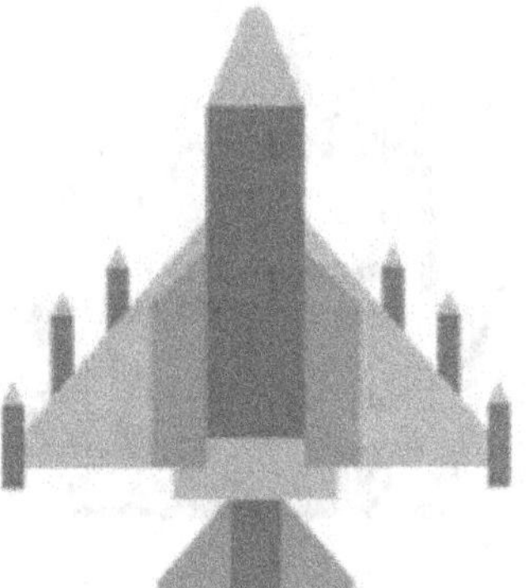

The jet is high-speed.

moto

मोटारसायकल

The motorcycle is on the road.

navire

जहाज

The ship is on the water.

métro

भुयारी मार्ग

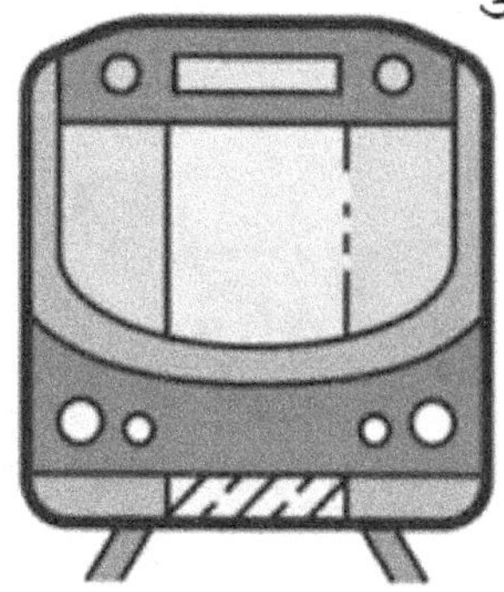

My mom goes on the subway to work.

taxi

टॅक्सी

The taxi has someone inside.

train

ट्रेन

The train is going slowly.

un camion

ट्रक

The truck has stuff in it.

asperges

शतावरी

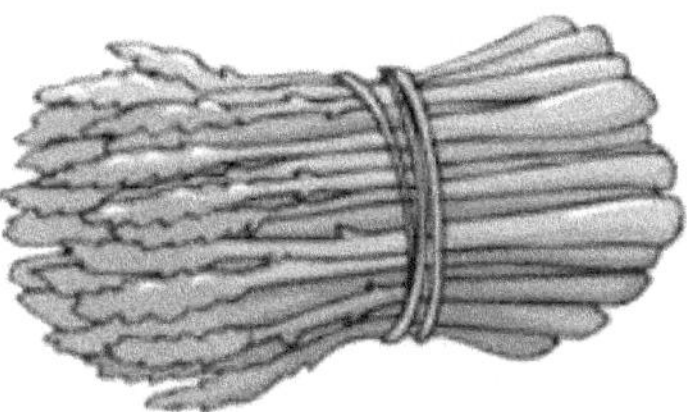

The asparagus is in a bundle.

des haricots

सोयाबीनचे

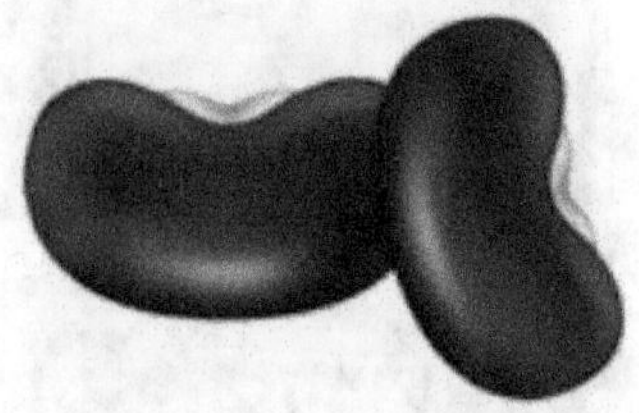

The beans are smooth.

brocoli

ब्रोकोली

The broccoli is dancing.

chou

कोबी

Bunnies like to eat cabbage.

carotte

गाजर

The carrots are very long.

céleri

भाजी किंवा कोशिंबीर बनवण्यासाठी
उपयुक्त अशी एक वनस्पती

The celery has lots of leaves.

blé

कॉर्न

Corn soup is delicious.

concombre

काकडी

The cucumbers are cut into pieces.

aubergine

वांगं

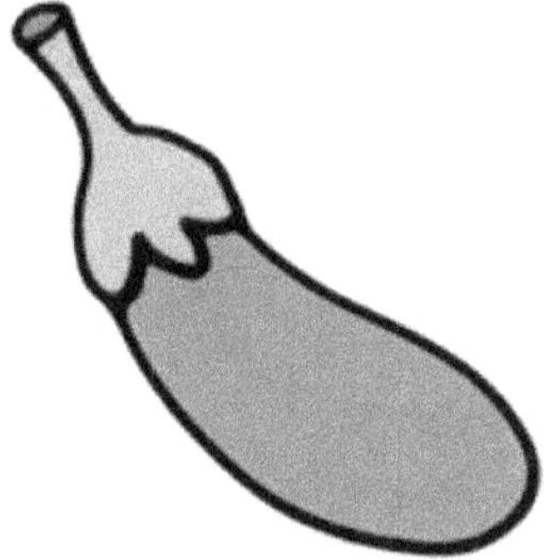

The eggplant is purple.

poivre vert

हिरवी मिरची

The green pepper is juicy.

salade

कोशिंबिरीसाठी वापरण्यात येणारा एक पाला व त्याचे झाड

The lettuce is all green.

oignon

कांदा

The onions make my eyes water.

pois

वाटाणे

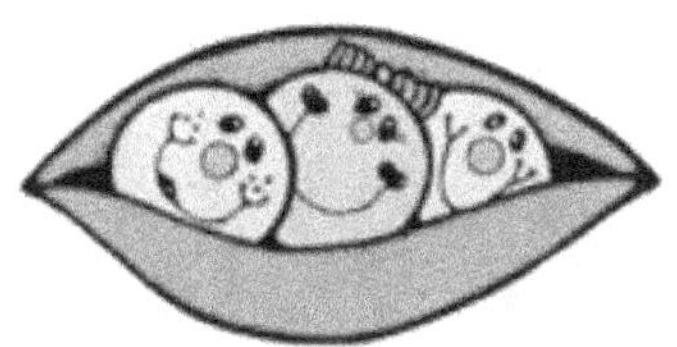

The peas are all in a pod.

patate

बटाटा

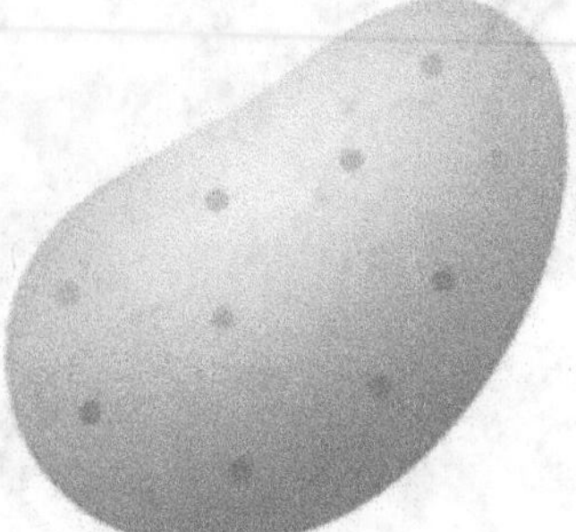

The potato is very shiny.

citrouille

भोपळा

The pumpkin is for Halloween.

un radis

मुळा

The radish is a type of vegetable.

épinard

पालक

The spinach is good with cheese.

patate douce

रताळे

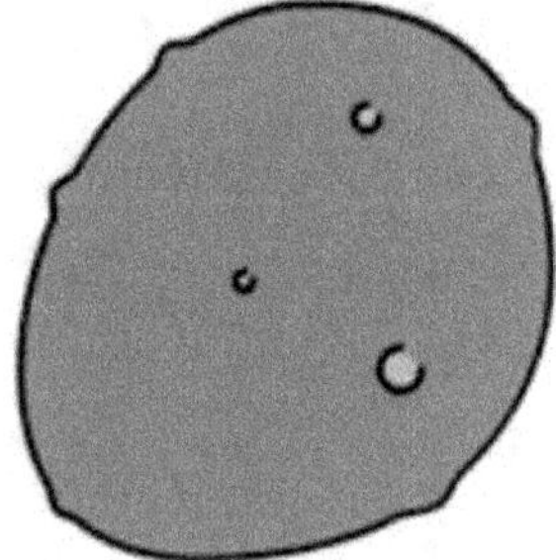

The sweet potato is quite sweet.

tomate

टोमॅटो

I don't like to eat tomatoes.

navet

सलगम नावाच कंद व त्याचे झाड

My mom bought some turnips.

nuageux

ढगाळ

The weather is cloudy today.

du froid

थंड

I like cold weather.

cool

मस्त

The temperature is cold today.

brumeux

धुके

The fog is so strong I can't see the city.

chaud

गरम

The fire is burning hot.

humide

दमट

It's so humid and wet today.

pluvieux

पावसाळी

It's raining very hard.

neigeux

हिमाच्छादित

Welcome to snow land!

orageux

वादळ

I hate the stormy weather.

ensoleillé

सनी

The sun is shining!

chaud

उबदार

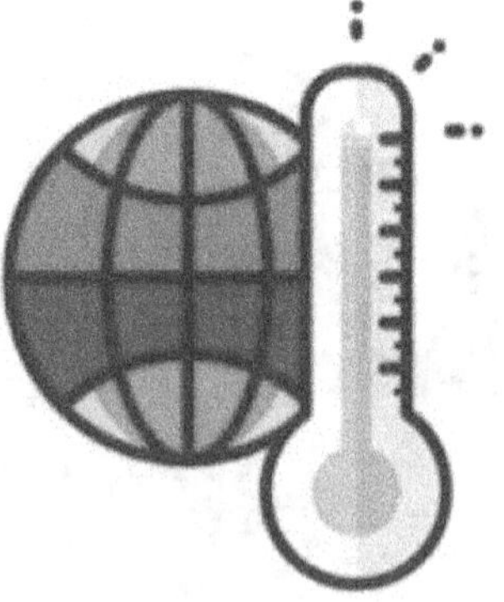

The whole world is warm today!

venteux

वादळी

The leaves are blowing away since it's so windy!

tante

काकू

My aunt is very nice to me.

frère

भाऊ

My brother is very fun to play with.

cousin

चुलतभाऊ

I love going to the playground with my cousin.

fille

मुलगी

I like to read books with my daughter.

père

वडील

My father is playing with me.

petite fille

नात

My granddaughter has blond hair.

grand-mère

आजी

My grandmother is very old and has glasses.

petit fils

नातू

My grandson and I are very excited today!

mère

आई

My mother likes to pick me up.

neveu

भाचा

My father's nephew is my cousin.

nièce

भाची

My niece is very good at playing ball.

sœur

बहीण

My sister is so pretty!

fils

मुलगा

My son likes to play with toy cars.

belle fille

सावत्र मुलगी

My stepdaughter likes the color orange.

belle-mère

सावत्र आई

My stepmother is pretty.

beau-fils

सौरा

This is my stepson, Greg.

oncle

काका

My uncle tells lots of funny jokes.

bol

वाडगा

The bowl has nothing inside.

tasse

कप

My mom drinks her coffee out of a cup.

plat

ताटली

That dish has a bone inside.

fourchette

काटा

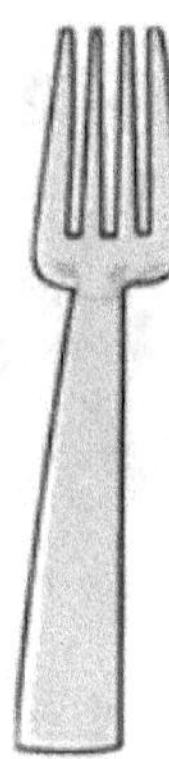

We have more spoons than forks.

verre

काच

I have a glass of water on my desk.

couteau

चाकू

I have a knife in my kitchen.

agresser

घोकंपट्टी

This mug of coffee is for my dad.

serviette de table

रुमाल

You can use the napkins to clean your hands.

poivre

मिरपूड

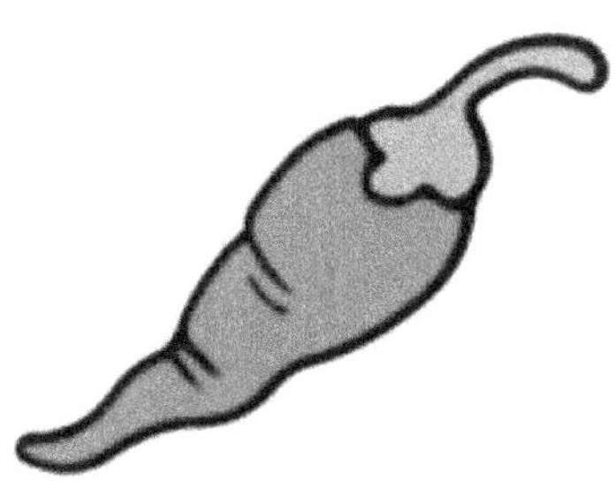

The pepper is very spicy.

lanceur

घागर

Pour yourself some lemonade from the pitcher.

assiette

प्लेट

Can you help me wash the plates?

salade

कोशिंबीर

The salad is very healthy for you.

sel

मीठ

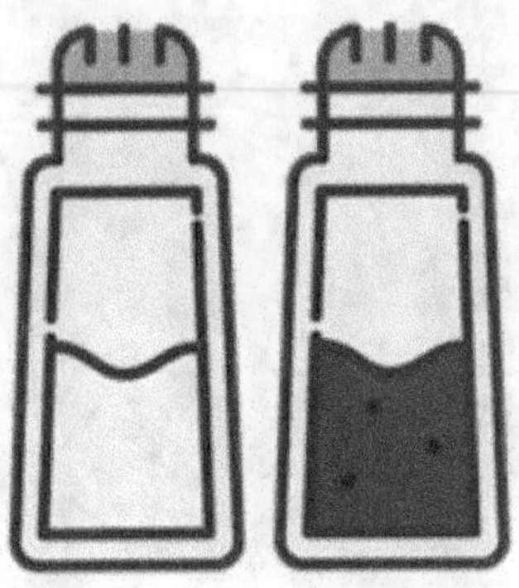

The salt tastes good with a few pinches of pepper.

soucoupe

बशी

The plate is for my cup.

cuillère

चमचा

I use a spoon to eat my rice.

sucre

साखर

The pack of sugar is very heavy.

dimanche

रविवारी

Sunday

Sunday is the day to go to Church!

lundi

सोमवार

Monday

Monday is the day to start school.

mardi

मंगळवार

Tuesday

We will go to the shops on Tuesday.

mercredi

बुधवार

Wednesday

Wednesday is hard to spell!

jeudi

गुरुवार

Thursday

Thursday is the fourth day of the week!

vendredi

शुक्रवार

Friday

My birthday is on Friday!

samedi

शनिवार

Saturday

Saturday is the weekend!

cuire

बेक करावे

The chef will bake a cake.

ébullition

उकळणे

I will boil the eggs.

griller

भांडण

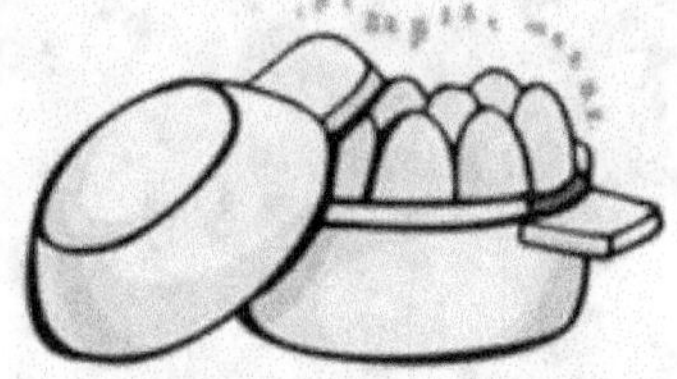

Broil is very yummy.

ouvre-boîte

सलामीवीर करू शकतो

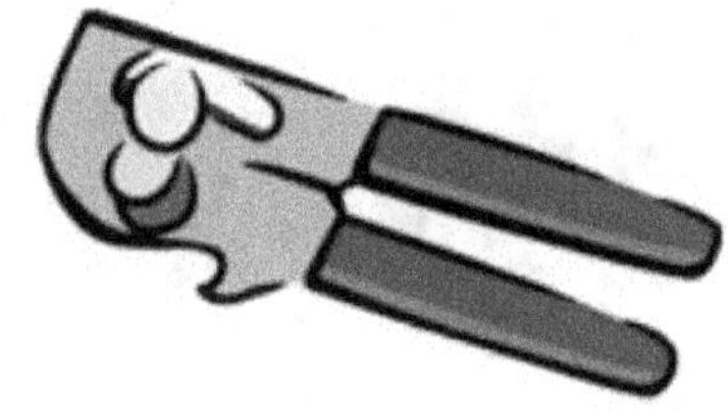

That can opener is used for opening cans.

frire

तळणे

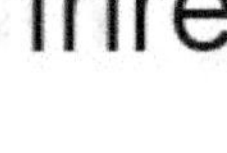

The pan can fry lots of things.

gril

लोखंडी जाळीची चौकट

We have a grill in our backyard.

tasse à mesurer

मोजण्याचे कप

My mom uses the measuring cup for baking.

cuillère à mesurer

मोजण्याचे चमचे

I use a measuring spoon to eat my dessert.

four micro onde

मायक्रोवेव्ह

The microwave is used to heat food.

bol à mélanger

मिक्सिंग वाडगा

She is using the mixing bowl to mix things.

serviettes en papier

कागदी टॉवेल्स

Dry your hands with paper towels.

poché aux œufs

अंडी पीच

The poach is put on noodles.

porte pot

भांडे धारक

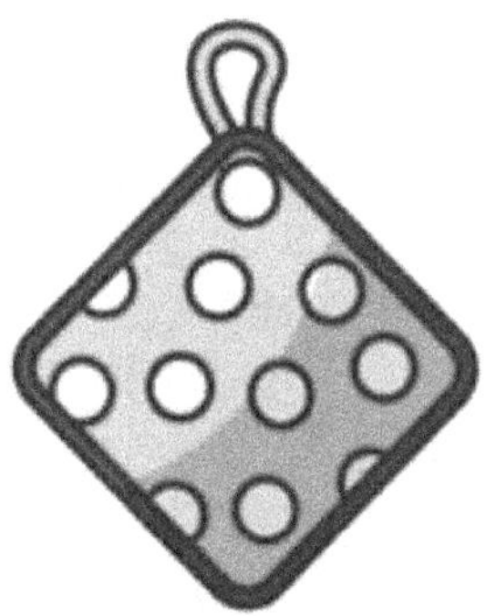

The potholder is soft.

rôti

भाजणे

The chef made roast chicken.

rouleau à pâtisserie

लाटणे

He is holding a rolling pin.

brouiller

ओरखडे

My mom is making scrambled eggs for breakfast.

mijoter

उकळण्याची

The simmer is rice today.

couteau

चाकू

The knife is sharp.

cuillère

चमचा

I eat my food with a spoon and fork.

spatule

बोथट

The spatula will help us flip the steak over.

vapeur

स्टीम

The steam is coming from the pot.

passoire

गाळणे

The strainer is used to strain stuff.

minuteur

टाइमर

I set my timer for 12:00.

fourchette

काटा

I have lots of metallic forks.

grille-pain

टोस्टर

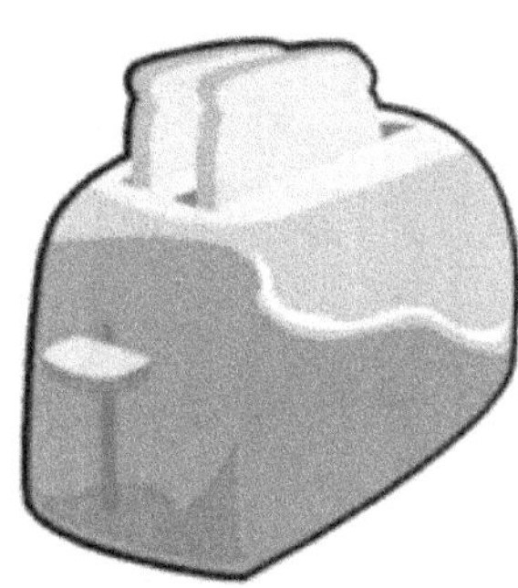

The toaster will toast my bread.

bouilloire

किटली

The kettle has tea inside.

réfrigérateur

रेफ्रिजरेटर

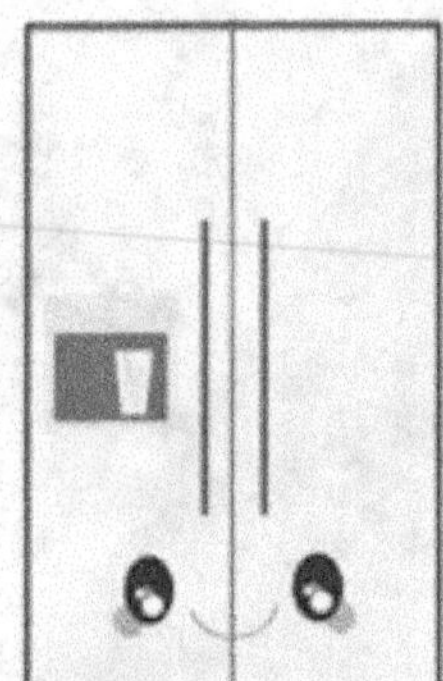

The refrigerator has lots of things inside.

mixeur

ब्लेंडर

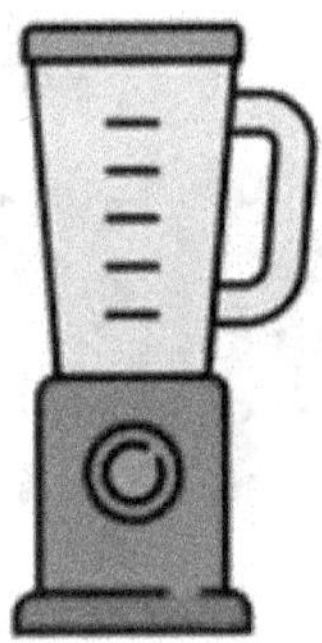

The blender will mix up my fruits.

cabinets

कॅबिनेट्स

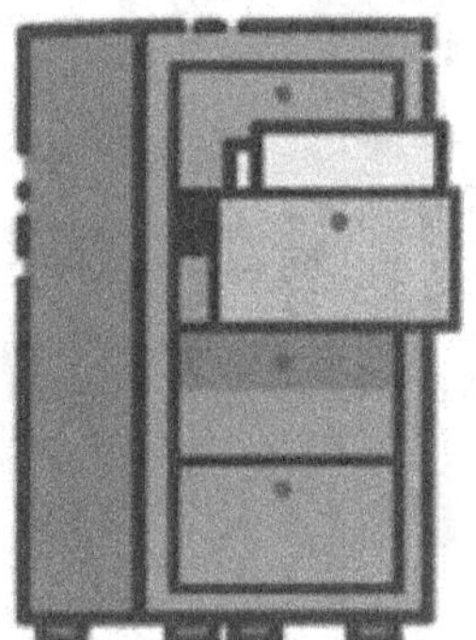

The cabinet has my paper inside.

placard

कपाट

The cupboard has lots of books.

four micro onde

मायक्रोवेव्ह

The microwave will heat my food.

arrière

परत

She has a slender back.

des joues

गाल

She kisses her mom on the cheek.

poitrine

छाती

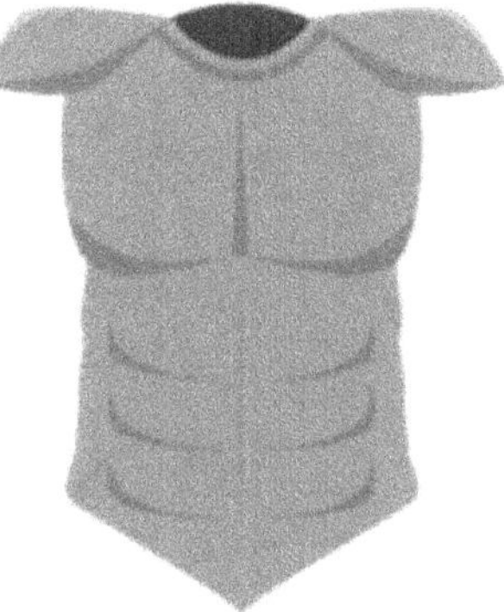

The armor is for your chest.

menton

हनुवटी

This is my chin!

oreilles

कान

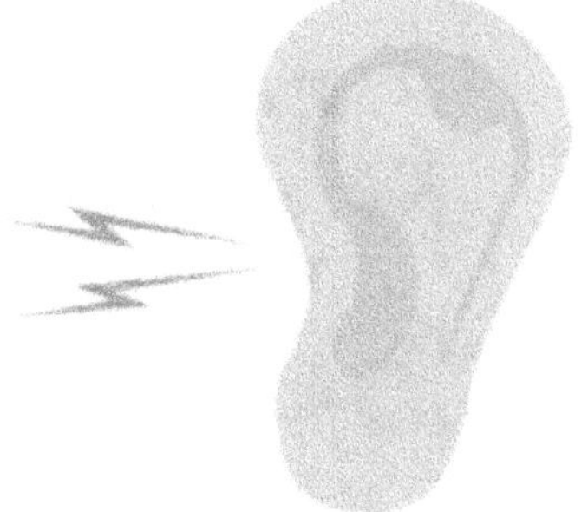

The ear is hearing something.

les sourcils

भुवया

The eyebrows are raised.

yeux

डोळे

The eyes are blue.

pieds

पाय

I have one pair of feet.

des doigts

बोटांनी

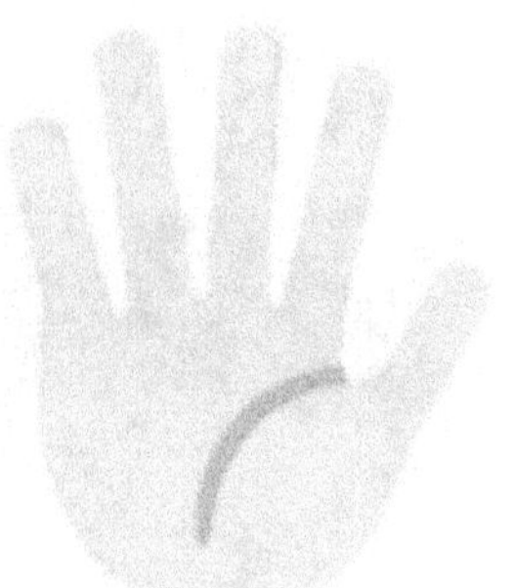

The fingers are waving at us.

pied

पाऊल

My foot has five fingers.

front

कपाळ

My brain is behind my forehead.

cheveux

केस

My hair is long and black.

mains

हात

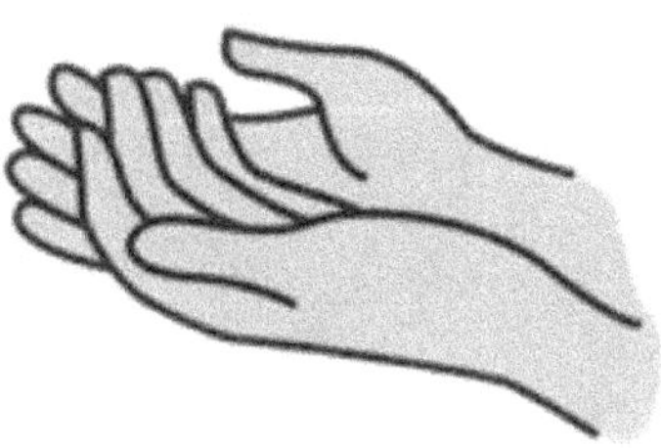

I will wash my hands in the sink.

tête

डोके

She has a big head.

les hanches

कूल्हे

The gorilla has his hands on his hips.

les genoux

गुडघे

She is begging on her knees.

jambes

पाय

The tiger has strong legs.

lèvres

ओठ

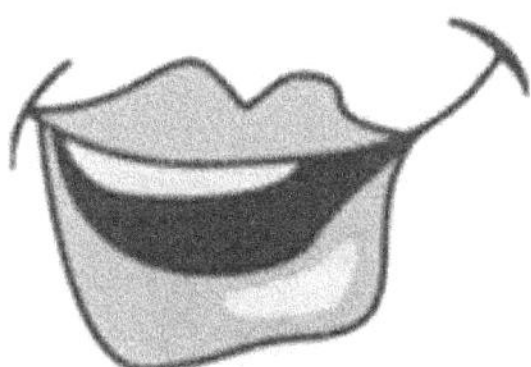

The lips have lipstick on.

bouche

तोंड

He is covering his mouth with his hand.

cou

मान

The necklace is very special to me.

nez

नाक

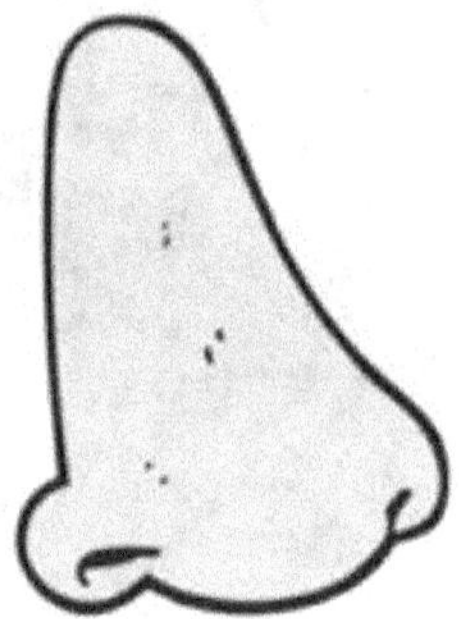

The nose smells something.

épaules

खांदे

He puts his hands on his shoulders.

estomac

पोट

He has a big stomach.

les dents

दात

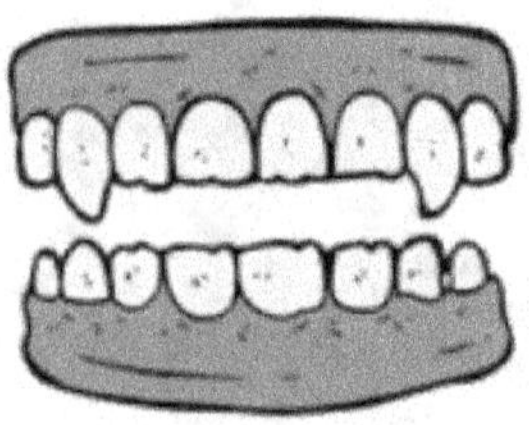

The teeth are clean and white.

gorge

घसा

He has a sore throat today.

les orteils

बोटांनी

My toes are small.

langue

जीभ

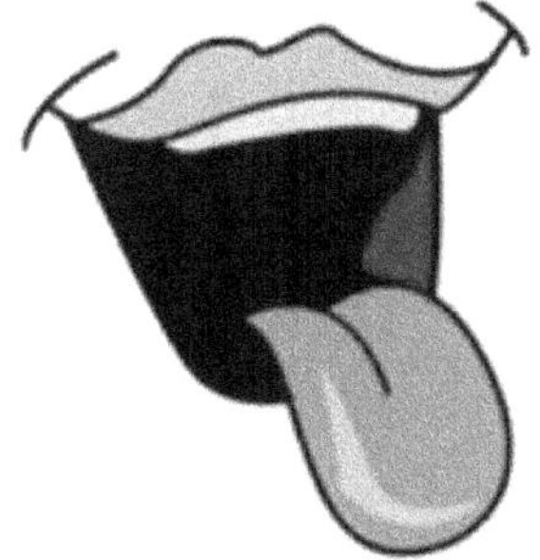

My tongue is licking ice cream.

dent

दात

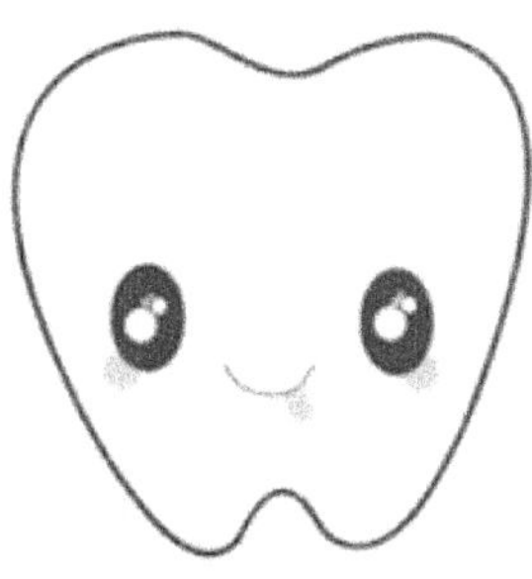

The tooth has big eyes.

taille

कंबर

He has his hands on his waist.

salopette

चौफेर

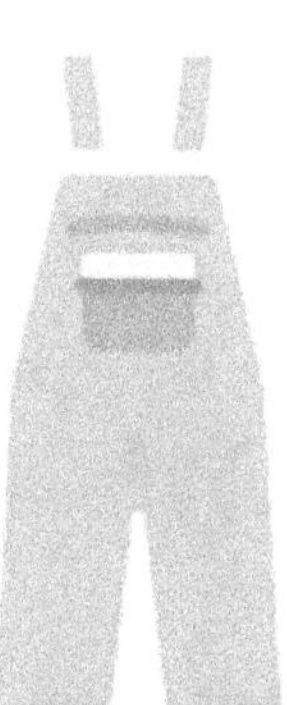

I bought these overalls for you!

mitaines

मिटेन्स

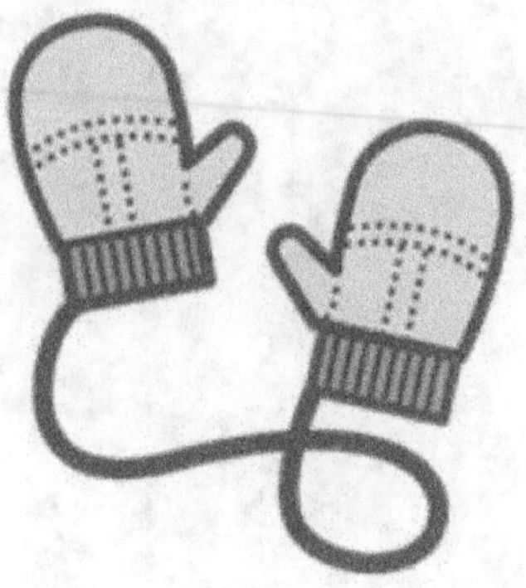

The mittens are very warm.

bonnet

बीनी

The beanie is for winter.

tablier

एप्रोन

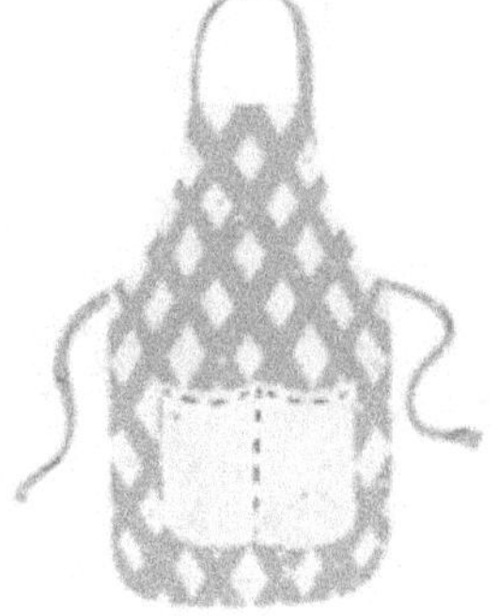

I wear my apron when I bake.

poupée

बाहुली

The doll is for my baby sister.

hochets

रॅटल्स

The rattle is for the baby.

jouet

टॉय

The toy is very fun.

couche

डायपर

The baby has to wear a diaper.

berceau

बॅसिनेट

She is sleeping in her bassinet.

bavoir

बीबी

My baby brother has to wear his bib when he is eating.

octogone

अष्टकोन

The octagon is saying okay!

triangle

त्रिकोण

The triangle has three corners.

carré

चौरस

Square

The square has four sides.

cercle

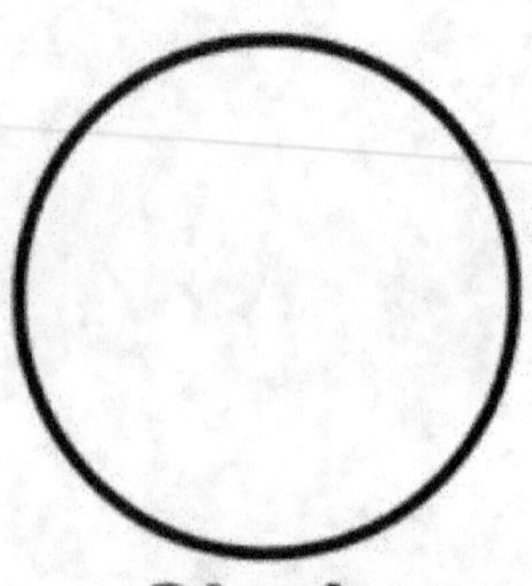

वर्तुळ

Circle

The circle is round.

ovale

ओव्हल

The oval shape looks like a circle.

cœur

हृदय

I drew a heart on my paper.

traverser

फुली

That sign is a cross.

la flèche

बाण

The arrow is pointing this way.

cube

घन

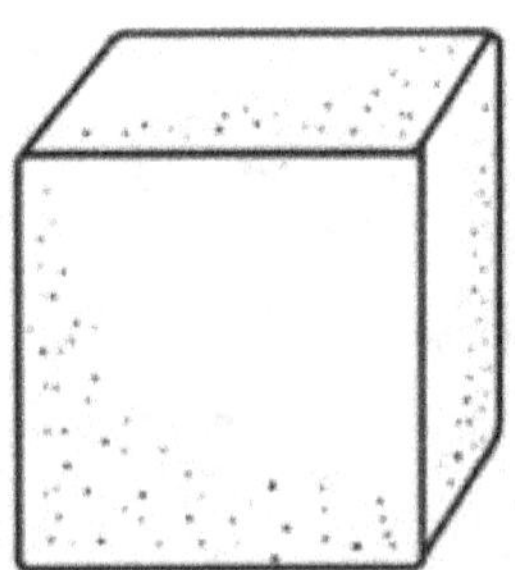

The cube is 3D.

étoile

तारा

The star is yellow and shiny.

tir à l'arc

धनुर्विद्या

The archery is where you aim.

badminton

बॅडमिंटन

My favorite sport is badminton.

criquet

क्रिकेट

I am very good at cricket.

bowling

गोलंदाजी

I got one pin down at bowling!

boxe

बॉक्सिंग

The boxing gloves are hot.

tennis

टेनिस

He can hit the ball in tennis.

faire de la planche a roulettes

स्केट बोर्डिंग

He skateboards to school.

planche de surf

सर्फबोर्डिंग

The shark loves surfing in the ocean.

le hockey

हॉकी

I like to play Ice hockey.

yoga

योग

He is closing his eyes and doing yoga.

épée

तलवार वाजवणे

They are fencing and dueling together.

aptitude

तंदुरुस्ती

She will do some fitness in the pool.

gymnastique

जिम्नॅस्टिक

He can do brilliant gymnastics.

karaté

कराटे

She is good at kicking in Karate.

volley-ball

व्हॉलीबॉल

She is holding a volleyball.

musculation

वजन उचल

The girl with brown hair can do weightlifting.

basketball

बास्केटबॉल

He can balance the ball with one finger in basketball.

base-ball

बेसबॉल

The little chick is in the finales at baseball.

le rugby

रग्बी

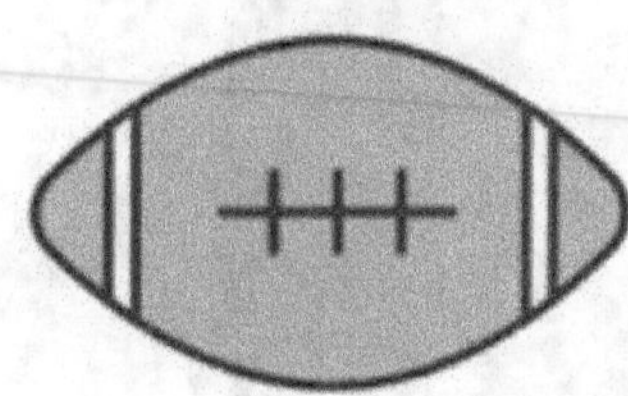

The rugby ball has white stripes.

lutte

कुस्ती

The sumo will compete in wrestling.

course de voitures

कार रेसिंग

He is number one for car racing.

cyclisme

सायकलिंग

He is peacefully cycling on the road.

fonctionnement

चालू आहे

He is running while listening to his earphones.

tennis de table

टेबल टेनिस

My brother and dad will play table tennis.

pêche

मासेमारी

He will go to the river to fish.

judo

ज्युडो

She has a red belt in Judo.

escalade

चढणे

He will climb the ladder.

tournage

शूटिंग

He is shooting the archery board.

le golf

गोल्फ

She is going to compete in the golf competition.

balade

राइड

He will ride his scooter.

asseyez-vous

खाली बसा

They are sitting down together.

se lever

उभे रहा

She likes to stand up.

bats toi

लढा

They are fighting over the book.

rire

हसणे

He is laughing so hard!

lis

वाचा

She read a picture book.

jouer

खेळा

He went to play on the slide.

ecoutez

ऐका

He listened for the ice cream cart.

pleurer

रडणे

He cried because he got a bad grade.

pense

विचार करा

He thought that the test would be hard.

chanter

गाणे

He sang for the concert.

regarder la télévision

टीव्ही पहा

He watched TV the whole night.

danse

नृत्य

She was a good dancer.

allumer

चालू करणे

The light is turned on.

éteindre

बंद कर

The light is turned off.

gagner

विन

He won the contest.

mouche

उडणे

The parrot can fly.

couper

कट

He was cutting his nails.

désinvolte

दूर फेकणे

He threw away the garbage.

dormir

झोपा

He slept soundly.

fermer

बंद

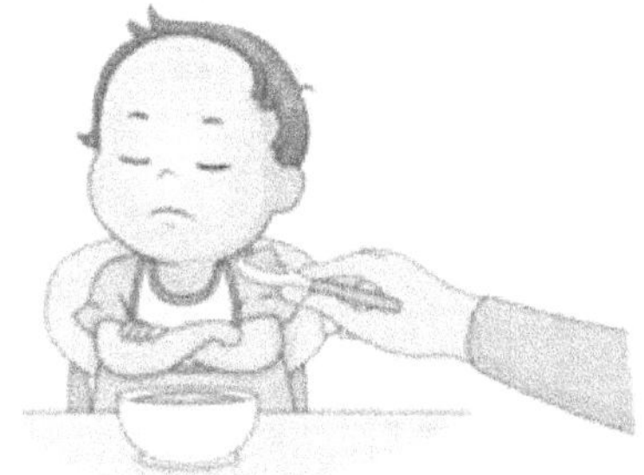

He closed his mouth shut.

ouvert

उघडा

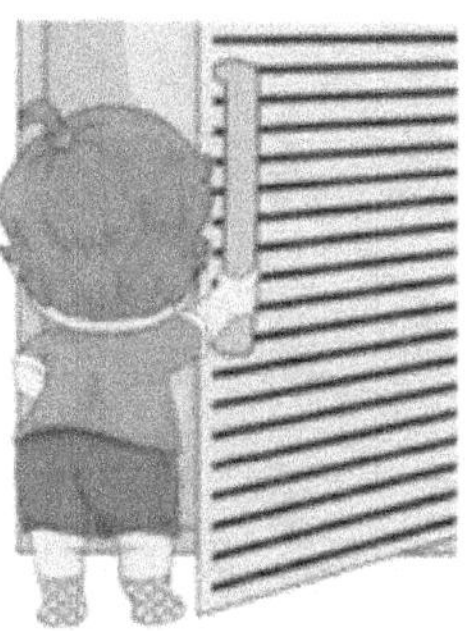

She opened the bathroom door.

écrire

लिहा

She wrote with a pencil.

donner

द्या

Santa gave her a present.

sauter

उडी

She had fun jumping.

manger

खा

The shark ate yummy ice cream.

boisson

पेय

The old British man drank tea.

cuisinier

कूक

The microwave cooked his soup.

lavage

धुवा

You need to remember to wash your hands.

attendre

थांबा

He was waiting for the bus.

montée

चढणे

She climbed a lot of mountains.

parler

चर्चा

Two best friends were talking together.

crawl

रेंगाळणे

The baby crawled on the floor.

rêver

स्वप्न

The Sloth dreamed about eating leaves.

creuser

खणणे

That strong man dug a swimming pool.

taper

टाळ्या

The baby clapped her hands.

tricoter

विणणे

She knits with the purple string.

coudre

शिवणे

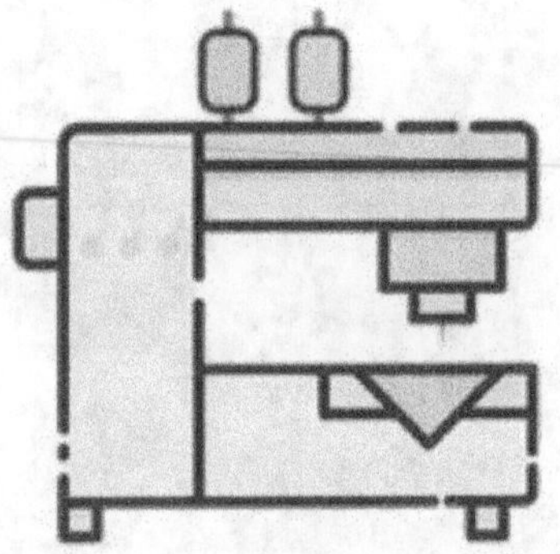

That is a sewing machine.

odeur

गंध

The perfume smelled great.

baiser

चुंबन

He kissed his mother.

étreinte

मिठी

They hugged each other.

ronfler

घोरणे

The tiger snored.

baigner

स्नान

He took a bath.

s'incliner

धनुष्य

He bowed to the judge.

peindre

रंग

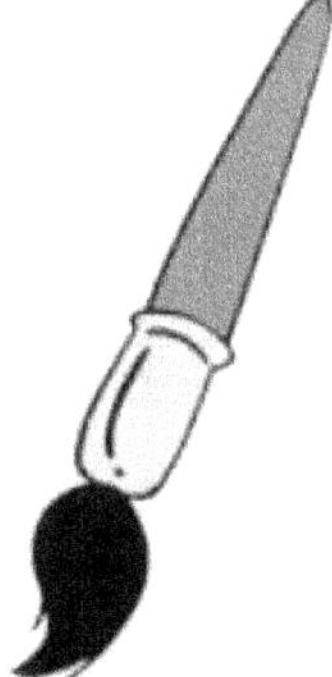

He painted a colorful picture.

se plonger

गोता

He dove to the deepest part of the ocean.

ski

स्की

The ski was expensive.

empiler

स्टॅक

The books are stacked high.

acheter

खरेदी करा

They bought cereal.

secouer

शेक

They shook hands together.

programmeur

प्रोग्रामर

He was a smart computer programmer.

vétérinaire

पशुवैद्य

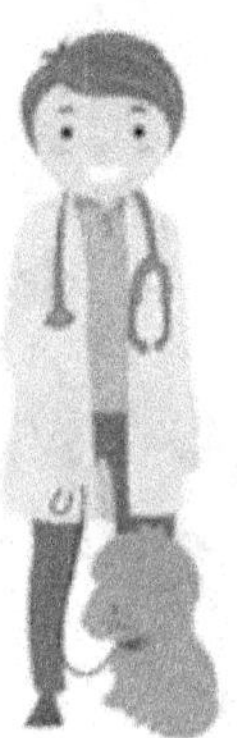

She is a veterinarian.

vendeur de rue

मार्ग विक्रेता

That street vendor sells hot dogs.

mineur

खाणकाम करणारा

That Miner will find gold.

prof

शिक्षक

The owl is the teacher.

groom

बेलबॉय

That Bellboy is fat.

orateur

स्पीकर

The chicken is a great Speaker.

boucher

खाटीक

The Butcher sells fish.

pharmacien

फार्मासिस्ट

That Pharmacist saved a person's life.

réceptionniste

रिसेप्शनिस्ट

He is a Receptionist.

politicien

राजकारणी

He wants to be a Politician.

guide touristique

सहल मार्गदर्शक

That Tour guide led us around Japan.

entrepreneur

उद्योजक

He is an Entrepreneur.

danseuse de ballet

बॅले नर्तक

She is training to be a Ballet dancer.

astronaute

अंतराळवीर

He is a great astronaut.

juge

न्यायाधीश

That Judge is always fair.

avocat

वकील

The lawyer is serious.

la caissière

रोखपाल

She is a cashier at the market.

conducteur de taxi

टॅक्सी चालक

He is a fast Taxi driver.

plombier

प्लंबर

That Plumber fixes toilets.

musicien

संगीतकार

She wants to be a Musician like her teacher.

chef

शेफ

The chef makes fast food.

boulanger

बेकर

That baker is a bread.

artiste

कलाकार

That Artist came from Italy.

acteur

अभिनेता

That actor is famous.

barman

बारकीपर

The Bartender works in a bar.

coiffeur

केशभूषा

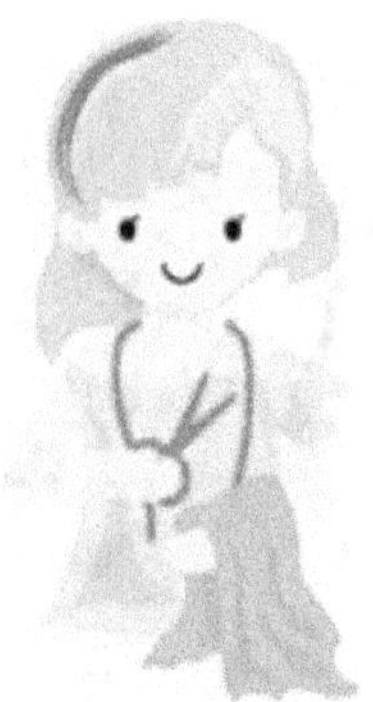

That girl is a Hairdresser.

évêques

बिशप

He is a Bishop.

opticien

ऑप्टिशियन

She went to an Optician.

fleuriste

फुलवाला

She is a great Florist.

écrivain

लेखक

He is a famous author.

comptable

लेखापाल

My accountant is loyal.

du vin

वाइन

That wine tastes good.

café

कॉफी

That coffee is bitter.

limonade

लिंबूपाला

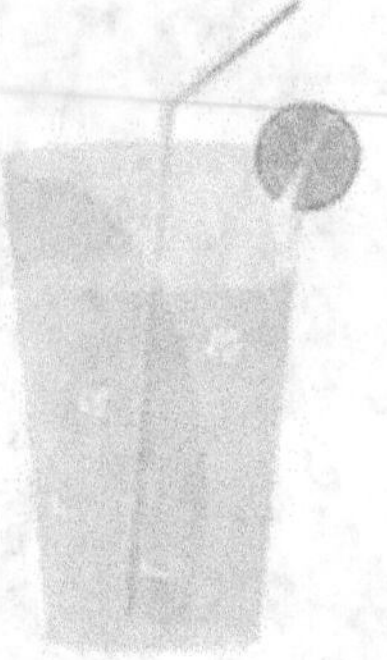

The lemonade is refreshing.

chocolat chaud

गरम चॉकलेट

I drink hot chocolate every day.

milk-shake

मिल्कशेक

The milkshake has whipped cream.

eau

पाणी

The water is not cold.

thé

चहा

The tea is hot.

lait

दूध

Milk is white.

bière

बीअर

The beer is foamy.

un soda

सोडा

The soda is fizzy.

smoothie

स्मूदी

The smoothie is a watermelon flavor.

milk-shake

मिल्कशेक

The milkshake has whipped cream.

lait de coco

नारळाचे दुध

The coconut milk is yummy.

du jus d'orange

संत्र्याचा रस

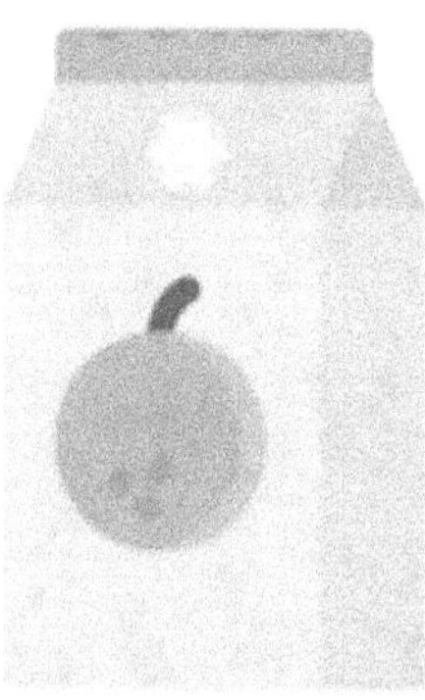

The orange juice is made from oranges.

cacao

कोको

The cocoa is sweet.

fromage

चीज

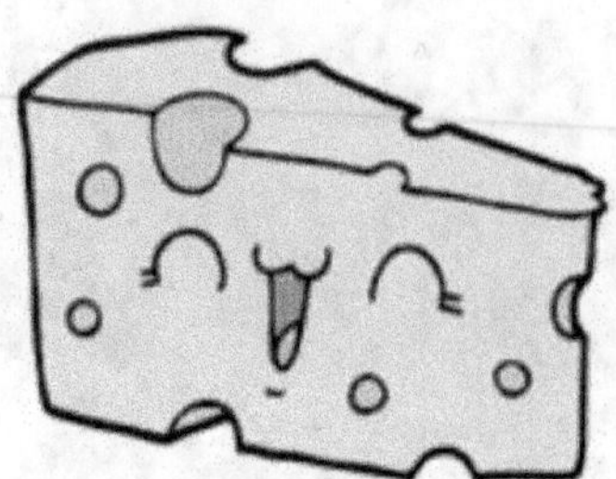

The cheese is creamy.

oeuf

अंडी

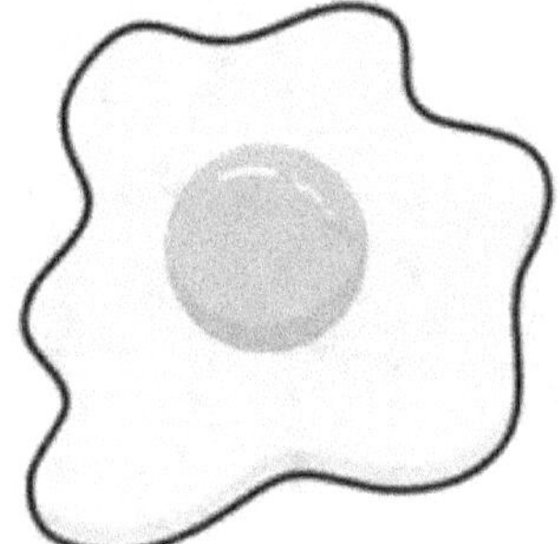

The egg is fried.

beurre

लोणी

The butter is put on bread.

margarine

मार्जरीन

Margarine looks like butter.

yaourt

दही

That yogurt is popular.

cottage cheese

कॉटेज चीज

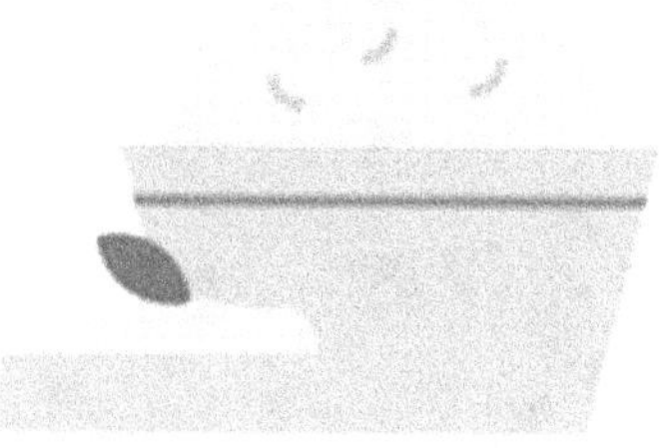

The cottage cheese is put on crackers.

crème glacée

आईसक्रीम

They have a triple scoop ice cream.

crème

मलई

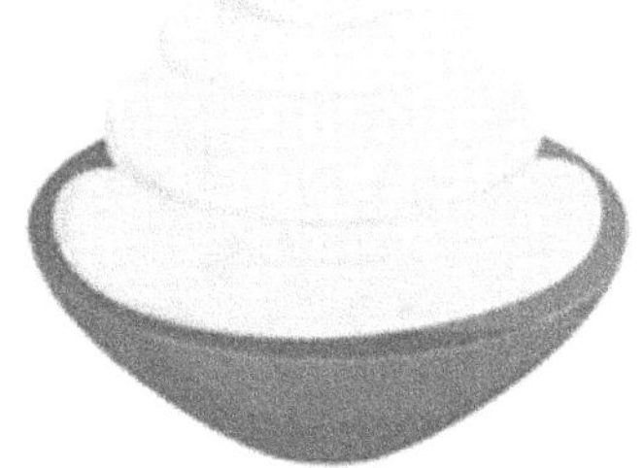

That is a lot of creams.

sandwich

सँडविच

That sandwich is healthy.

saucisse

सॉसेज

Americans love sausages.

hamburger

हॅमबर्गर

That hamburger looks happy.

hot-dog

गरम कुत्रा

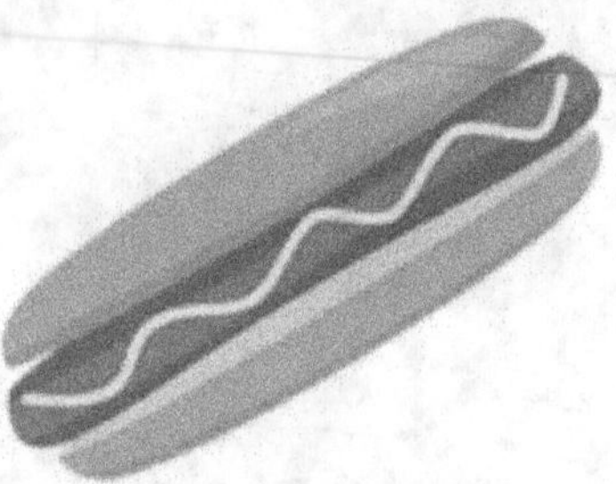

That hot dog has mustard on it.

pain

भाकरी

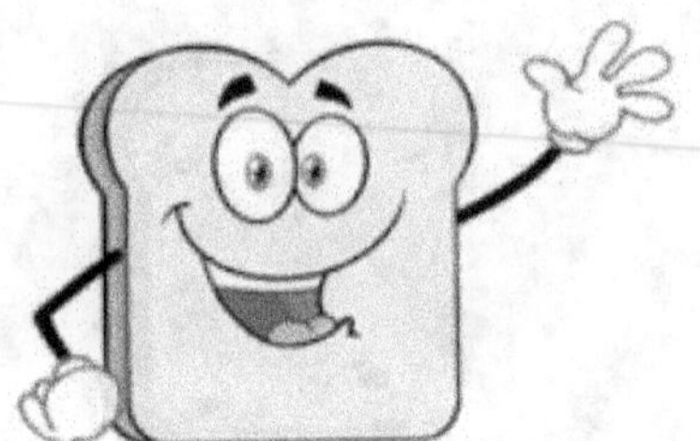

That bread is saying hello.

pizza

पिझ्झा

That pizza is cheesy.

steak

स्टेक

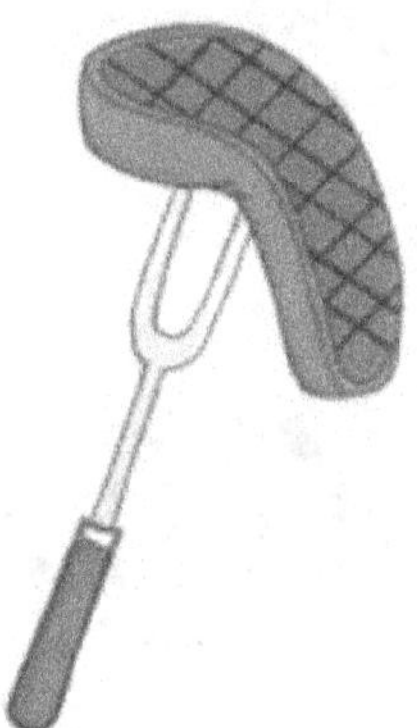

The steak was grilled.

poulet rôti

भाजलेला कोंबडी

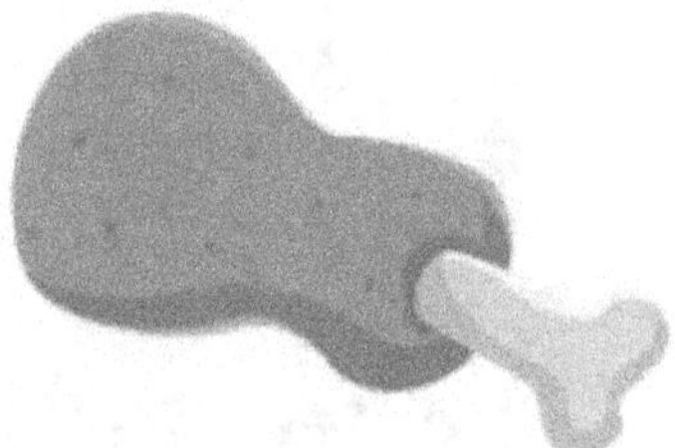

Roast Chicken is delicious.

poisson

मासे

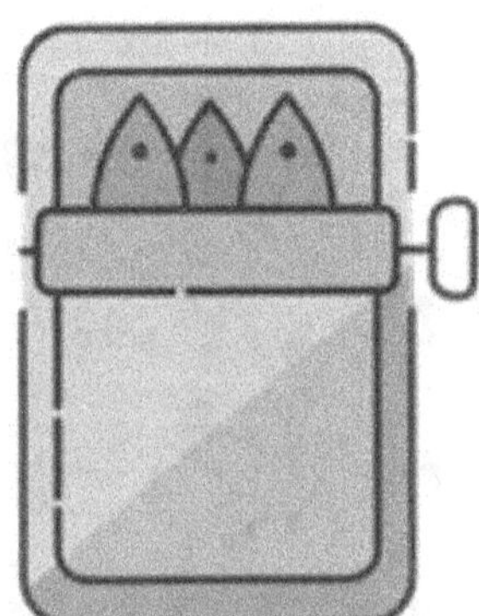

You can buy canned fish in the market.

fruit de mer

सीफ़ूड

Lobster is expensive seafood.

jambon

हॅम

Ham can be put in sandwiches.

kebab

कबाब

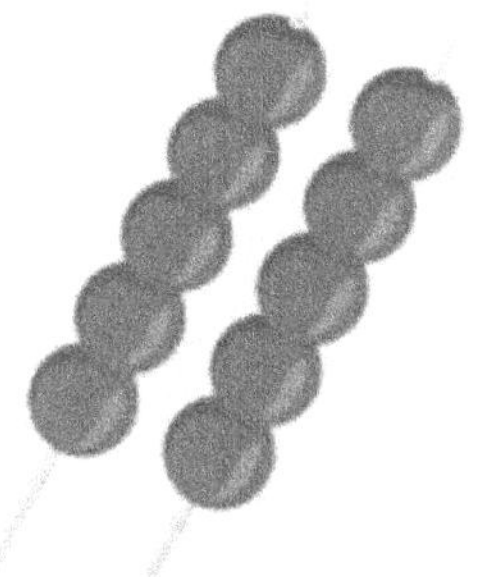

Kebab is a delicacy in America.

bacon

खारवून वाळवलेले डुकराचे मांस

That bacon is smiling.

crème fraîche

आंबट मलई

You can dip your chips in sour cream.

vache

गाय

Cows are black and white.

lapin

ससा

That rabbit is fun to play with.

canard

बदक

That duck is content.

crevette

कोळंबी मासा

The shrimp has six legs.

porc

डुक्कर

That pig is pink and fat.

abeille

मधमाशी

The bee has a stinger.

chèvre

बकरी

That goat has a white horn.

crabe

खेकडा

The crab has two big pincers.

cerf

हरीण

That deer is sleeping.

dinde

तुर्की

The turkey has a giant tail.

colombe

पारवा

That dove is carrying a plant.

mouton

मेंढी

That sheep has fluffy wool.

poisson

मासे

That fish has colorful fins.

poulet

चिकन

That chicken is waking everybody up.

cheval

घोडा

The horse has a red mane.

chaise

खुर्ची

That wing chair is yellow.

meuble tv

टीव्ही स्टँड

The TV stand can hold books.

canapé

सोफा

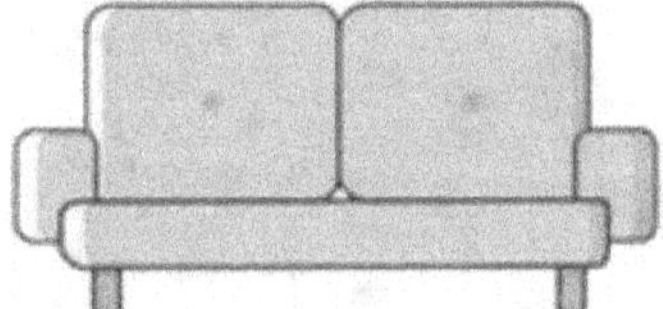

The sofa is comfortable to sit on.

coussins

उश्या

The cushion helps soften your seat.

téléphone

दूरध्वनी

The telephone is ringing.

télévision

दूरदर्शन

That television is big.

haut-parleurs

स्पीकर्स

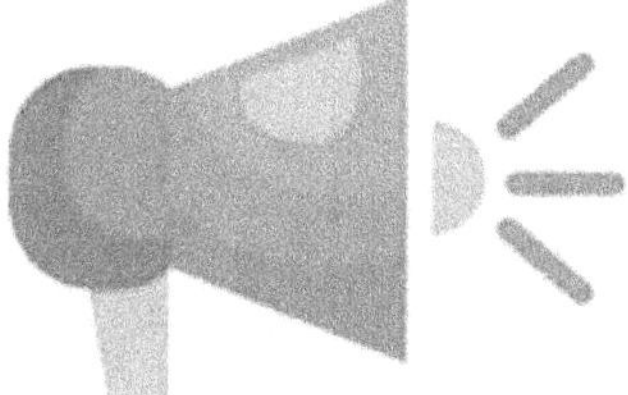

That speaker is used to increase the volume.

table d'appoint

साइड टेबल

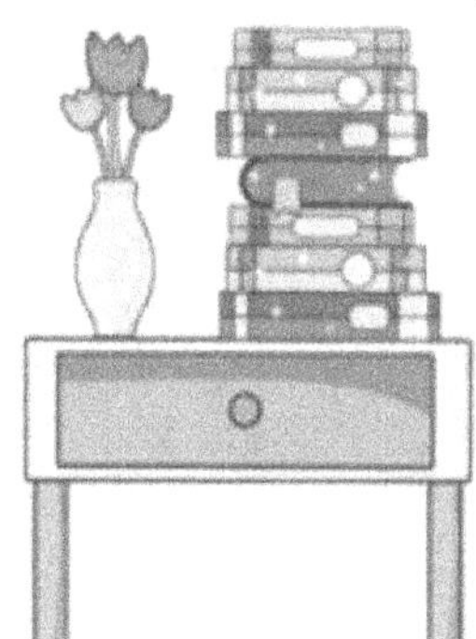

That end table is sparkling clean.

service à thé

चहाचा सेट

That tea set is from China.

cheminée

फायरप्लेस

The fireplace makes me warm.

télécommandes

रिमोट

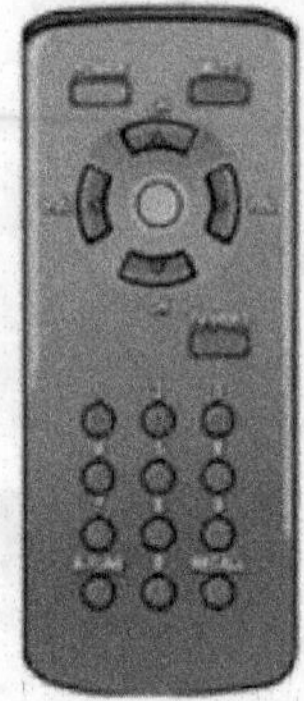

The remote has lots of buttons.

ventilateur électrique

विद्युत फॅन

The fan is blowing wind.

lampadaire

मजला दिवा

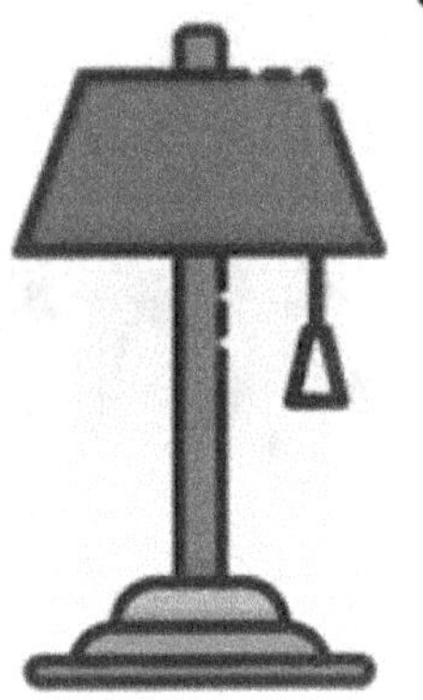

The floor lamp is very tall.

tapis

कार्पेट

The carpet is soft and silky.

bureaux

डेस्क

The table is made of wood.

stores

आंधळे

I will pull the blinds down.

rideaux

पडदे

She opened the curtains.

image

चित्र

The picture is about the mountains and the sky.

vase

फुलदाणी

The roses are all in a vase.

l'horloge

घड्याळ

The alarm clock is beeping.

oreiller

उशी

The pillow is pink and yellow.

cintre

हॅट हॅन्गर

The hat stand has only one hat on it.

mettre la table

ड्रेसिंग टेबल

I have made up on my dressing table.

lampe de table

टेबल दिवा

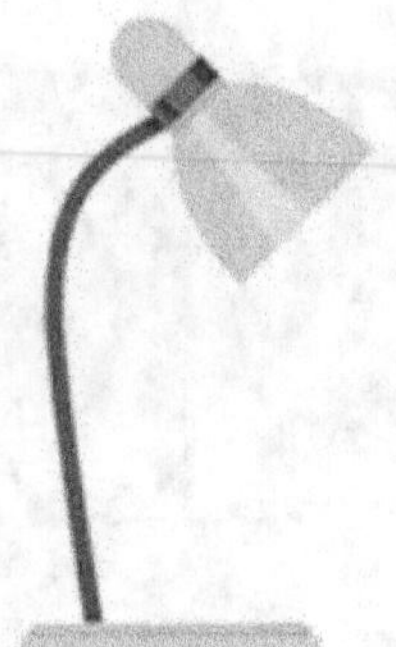

The table lamp will help me see in the dark.

miroir

आरसा

The mirror is very tall.

planche a repasser

इस्त्रीसाठी बोर्ड

Don't touch the ironing board, it's hot!

boîte avec tiroir

ड्रॉवर बॉक्स

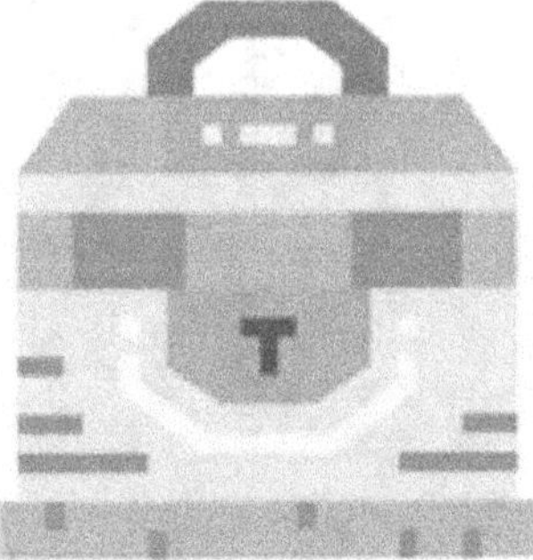

You can keep your clothes in the hope chest.

table de chevet

पलंगाकडचा टेबल

The nightstand has my lamp on it.

lit

बेड

The bed is charming.

climatisation

वातानुकूलित

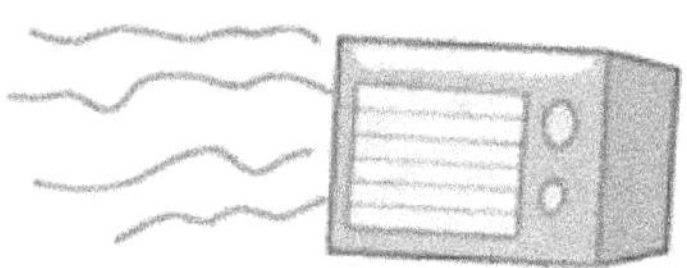

The air conditioner is cold.

cruche

जग

The measuring jug has nothing inside.

dentifrice

टूथपेस्ट

The toothpaste is mint flavored.

brosse à dents

दात घासण्याचा ब्रश

The toothbrush has toothpaste on it.

savon

साबण

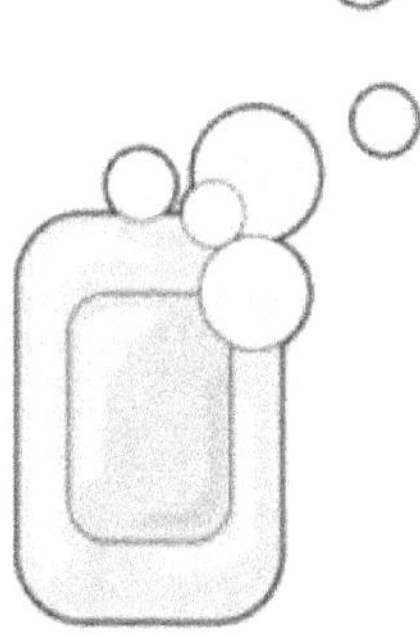

The soap is very bubbly.

pince à linge

क्लोथस्पीन

The clothespin will clip my clothes.

cintre

हँगर

The hanger is hanging my boots.

sèche-cheveux

केस ड्रायर

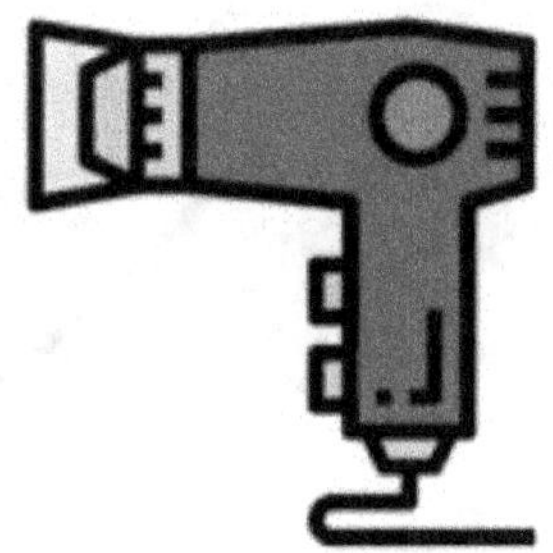

The hairdryer will blow my hair.

shampooing

शैम्पू

The shampoo is used to clean your hair.

bulle

बबल

The bubbles are very fun to play in.

brosse

ब्रश

She is brushing her hair with the brush.

papier toilette

टॉयलेट पेपर

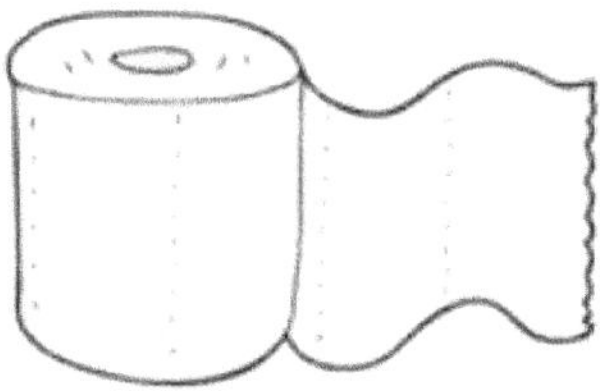

The toilet paper is used to dry your hands.

serviette

टॉवेल

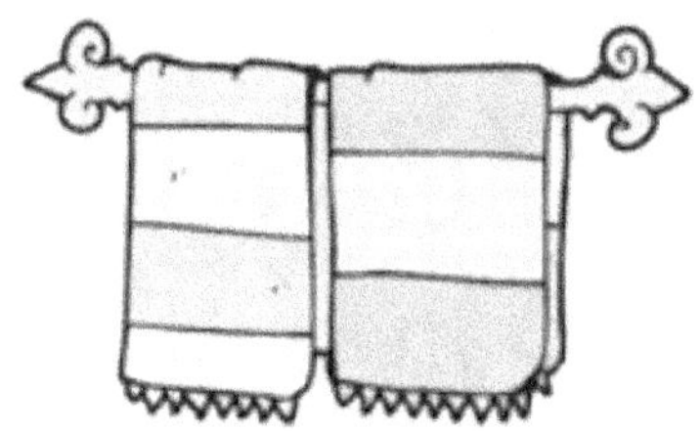

We have two towels on the rack.

corde à linge

क्लोथस्लाइन

My shirt is hanging on the clothesline.

douche

शॉवर

The shower is spraying water.

baignoire

बाथटब

The bathtub is comfortable.

lessive

लॉन्ड्री डिटर्जंट

The laundry detergent is used with the washing machine.

seau

बादली

Can you help me fill up the bucket?

vadrouilles

मोप्स

The mop is used for mopping the floor.

savon liquide

द्रव साबण

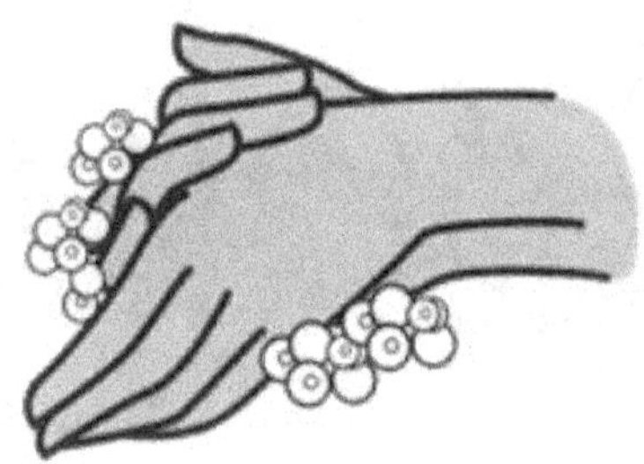

I use soapy water to wash my hands.

lessive en poudre

धुण्याची साबण पावडर

I will scoop up the washing powder.

sac poubelle

कचरा पिशवी

The trash bag is full of trash.

poubelle

कचरा कॅन

You have only to put recylcle trash in the trash can.

les puits

बुडणे

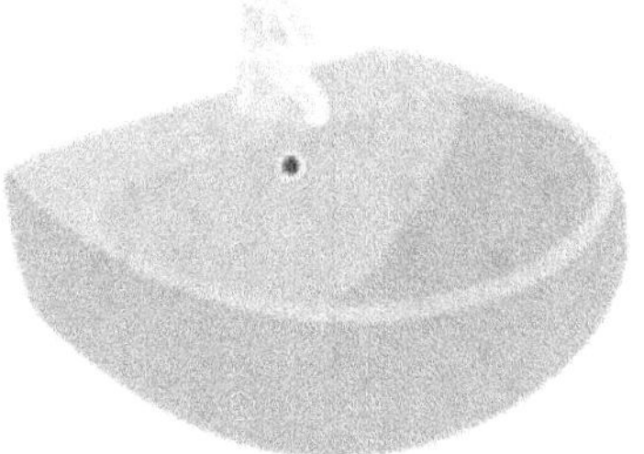

You should wash your hands in the sink.

cuvette des toilettes

टॉयलेट वाडगा

She let her bunny use the toilet.

machine à laver

वॉशिंग मशीन

The washing machine wash your clothes.

panier à linge

धुतलेले कपडे ठेवण्याची टोपली

She is putting all the clothes into the laundry basket.

le rasoir

वस्तरा

He uses the razor to shave his beard.

rasoir électrique

विद्युत वस्तरा

The electric razor works faster than the normal one.

crème à raser

दाढी करण्याची क्रीम

The shaving cream is fluffy.

bain de bouche

माउथवॉश

The mouthwash smells very lovely.

coton-tige

सूती कळी

Q-tip can be used for many things.

brosse à cheveux

केसांचा ब्रश

She brushes her hair with her hairbrush.

peigne

कंघी

Her dad will comb her hair for her.

nettoyant

क्लीन्सर

Put the cap back on the cleanser bottle.

échelle

स्केल

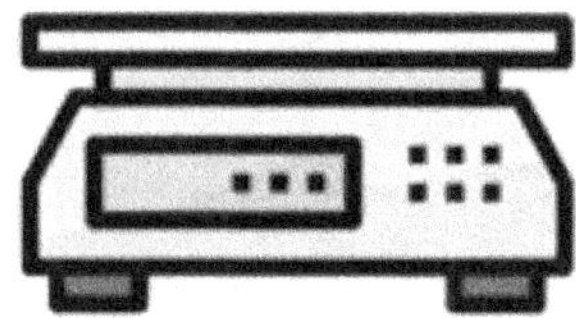

You can measure things on the scale.

papier de soie

हात पुसायचा पातळ कागद

The tissue is on the counter.

jouets de bain

आंघोळीची खेळणी

The little duck is a bath toy.

robinet

नळ

The faucet is broken.

miroir

आरसा

He is looking in the mirror.

tapis de bain

बाथरूम रग

The bath mat is purple and yellow.